W9-CBE-320

I I Voiced (Word) **Unit A**	**Mm** /mmm/ **Monkey** Continuous Voiced **Unit B**	**Ss** /sss/ **Snake** Continuous Unvoiced **Unit 1**	**Ee** /eee/ **Emu** Continuous Voiced (Long) **Unit 2**	**ee** /eeee/ **Bee** Continuous Voiced (Long) **Unit 2**	**Mm** /mmm/ **Monkey** Continuous Voiced **Unit 3**
Aa /aaa/ **Ant** Continuous Voiced (Short) **Unit 4**	**Dd** /d/ **Dinosaur** Quick Voiced (not duh) **Unit 5**	**th** /ththth/ **the** Continuous Voiced **Unit 6**	**Nn** /nnn/ **Nest** Continuous Voiced **Unit 7**	**Tt** /t/ **Turkey** Quick Unvoiced (not tuh) **Unit 8**	**Ww** /www/ **Wind** Continuous Voiced (woo) **Unit 9**
Ii /iii/ **Insects** Continuous Voiced (Short) **Unit 10**	**Th** /Ththth/ **The** Continuous Voiced **Unit 10**	**Hh** /h/ **Hippo** Quick Unvoiced (not huh) **Unit 11**	**Cc** /c/ **Cat** Quick Unvoiced (not cuh) **Unit 12**	**Rr** /rrr/ **Rabbit** Continuous Voiced **Unit 13**	**ea** /eaeaea/ **Eagle** Continuous Voiced (Long) **Unit 13**
Sh/sh /shshsh/ **Sheep** Continuous Unvoiced **Unit 14**	**Kk, -ck** /k/ **Kangaroo** Quick Unvoiced (not kuh) **Unit 15**	**oo** /oooo/ **Moon** Continuous Voiced (Long) **Unit 16**	**ar** /ar/ **Shark** Voiced (R-Controlled) **Unit 17**	**Wh/wh** /wh/ **Whale** Quick Voiced **Unit 18**	**Ee** /ĕĕĕ/ **Engine or Ed** Continuous Voiced (Short) **Unit 19**
-y /-yyy/ **Fly** Continuous Voiced (Long) **Unit 20**	**Ll** /lll/ **Letter** Continuous Voiced **Unit 21**	**Oo** /ooo/ **Otter** Continuous Voiced (Short) **Unit 22**	**Bb** /b/ **Bat** Quick Voiced (not buh) **Unit 23**	**all** /all/ **Ball** Voiced **Unit 23**	**Gg** /g/ **Gorilla** Quick Voiced (not guh) **Unit 24**
Ff /fff/ **Frog** Continuous Unvoiced **Unit 25**	**Uu** /uuu/ **Umbrella** Continuous Voiced (Short) **Unit 26**	**er** /er/ **Sister** Voiced (R-Controlled) **Unit 27**	**oo** /oo/ **Book** Voiced (Short) **Unit 27**	**Yy** /y-/ **Yarn** Quick Voiced **Unit 28**	**Aa** /a/ **Ago** Voiced (Schwa) **Unit 28**
Pp /p/ **Pig** Quick Unvoiced (not puh) **Unit 29**	**ay** /ay/ **Hay** Voiced **Unit 29**	**Vv** /vvv/ **Volcano** Continuous Voiced **Unit 30**	**Qu/qu** /qu/ **Quake** Quick Unvoiced **Unit 31**	**Jj** /j/ **Jaguar** Quick Voiced (not juh) **Unit 32**	**Xx** /ksss/ **Fox** Continuous Unvoiced **Unit 33**
or /or/ **Horn** Voiced (R-Controlled) **Unit 33**	**Zz** /zzz/ **Zebra** Continuous Voiced **Unit 34**	**a_e** /a_e/ **Cake** Bossy E Voiced (Long) **Unit 34**	**-y** /-y/ **Baby** Voiced **Unit 35**	**i_e** /i_e/ **Kite** Bossy E Voiced (Long) **Unit 35**	**ou** /ou/ **Cloud** Voiced **Unit 36**
ow /ow/ **Cow** Voiced **Unit 36**	**Ch/ch** /ch/ **Chicken** Quick Unvoiced **Unit 37**	**ai** /ai/ **Rain** Voiced (Long) **Unit 37**	**igh** /igh/ **Flight** Voiced (Long) **Unit 38**	**o_e** /o_e/ **Bone** Bossy E Voiced (Long) **Unit 38**	**ir** /ir/ **Bird** Voiced (R-Controlled) **Unit 38**

Mammals in Winter

Teacher's Guide

Read Well 1 · Unit 13

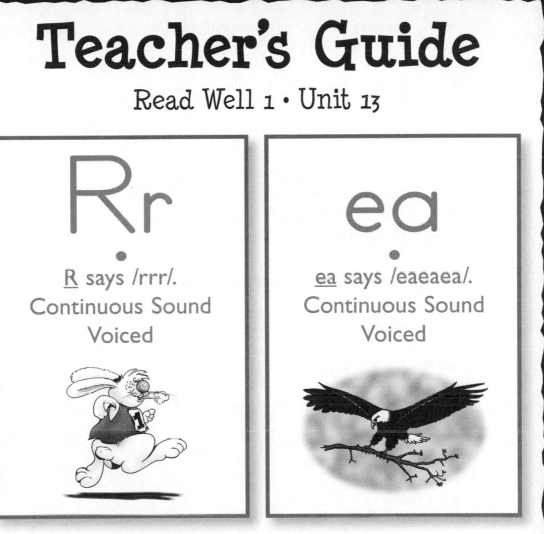

Rr

R says /rrr/.
Continuous Sound
Voiced

ea

ea says /eaeaea/.
Continuous Sound
Voiced

Critical Foundations in Primary Reading

Marilyn Sprick, Lisa Howard, Ann Fidanque, Shelley V. Jones

Copyright 2007 (Second Edition) Sopris West Educational Services. All rights reserved.

ISBN 13-digit: 978-1-59318-411-7   ISBN 10-digit: 1-59318-411-5   131852/2-13

12 13 14 15 16 RRDHRBVA 17 16 15 14 13

Table of Contents
Unit 13
Mammals in Winter

Introduction
Mammals in Winter

Story Notes

What do different animals do when the wind grows cold and snow covers the ground? Some hide in the mud. Some crawl under rocks. Where should a little rabbit hide? Where would a big bear sleep?

Recommended Read Aloud

For reading outside of small group instruction

The Mitten retold by Jan Brett

Fiction • Narrative, Problem Solution

Nicki's grandmother helps him prepare for winter by knitting him a pair of beautiful white mittens. When Nicki drops one of his mittens, the animals of the forest find that the mitten is indeed a warm and cozy place to get away from the cold of winter. This Ukrainian folktale can be enjoyed at many levels as children search the delightful illustrations for clues about what will happen next.

Read Well Connection

In *The Mitten*, students hear a fictional account of how a child's mitten becomes a warm winter haven for little forest animals. Similarly, in the *Read Well* stories, children read winter tales about a rabbit trying to prepare for winter and a bear that gets stuck half in and half out of his winter abode.

NOTE FROM THE AUTHORS

It is an act of kindness when you teach to mastery. A firm foundation ensures future success and builds self-confidence.

New and Important Objectives
A Research-Based Reading Program
Just Right for Young Children

Oral Language
Phonemic Awareness
Phonics
Fluency
Vocabulary
Comprehension

◆◆ Oral Language

Language patterns can be found in Stretch and Shrink, Smooth and Bumpy Blending, Sounding Out Smoothly, and Dictation. Continue practice throughout the day. Prompt students who would benefit from additional oral language practice to use the language patterns during instruction. (See page 10 for a list of the Unit 13 Oral Language Patterns.)

Phonemic Awareness

Isolating Beginning, Middle, Ending Sounds,
Segmenting, Blending, Manipulating, Rhyming, Onset and Rime

Phonics

Letter Sounds and Combinations

★*Rr,* ★*ea*
★*tr-,* ★*thr-*
Review • *Ss, Ee, ee, Mm, Aa, Dd, th, Nn, Tt, Ww, Ii, Th, Hh, Cc*

Pattern Words

★*cats,* ★*dam,* ★*deer,* ★*eat,* ★*ham,* ★*hams,* ★*hear,* ★*heat,* ★*meat,* ★*mid,* ★*near,* ★*neat,* ★*ram,* ★*ran,* ★*rat,* ★*rats,* ★*Rats,* ★*read,* ★*rear,* ★*rid,* ★*seat,* ★*Sid,* ★*swam,* ★*sweets,* ★*Tad,* ★*three,* ★*Three,* ★*tram,* ★*treat,* ★*tree*

Review • *am, and, Can, can't, cat, Cat, deer, did, didn't, had, he, hid, him, Hiss, in, mad, man, meet, need, sad, sat, see, seed, sit, sweet, swim, Tee hee, that, This, Tim, wind*

Tricky Words

★*want,* ★*wants*
Review • *a, as, has, hasn't, his, His, I, is, isn't, said, the, The, was, wasn't, with*

R says /rrr/.
Racing rabbit,
/R/, /r/, /rrr/.

Continuous Sound
(not ruh)

◆◆ = Oral language patterns   ★ = New in this unit

2

Comprehension

Comprehension Strategies
Priming Background Knowledge, Making Connections, Predicting, Identifying, Explaining, Inferring, Responding, Visualizing, Summarizing, Sequencing

Story Elements
Title, Who (Character), Problem, What (Action), Want (Goal)

Story Vocabulary
★Rabbit, ★Bear, ★Rat

Text Structure
Beginning, Middle, End

Genre
Fiction • Narrative With Factual Content

Lesson
★Each animal has its own way of adapting to its environment.

Written Response
Sentence Copying, Sentence Illustration, Sentence Completion, Sentence Comprehension—Multiple Choice

Fluency

Accuracy, Expression, Rate

Daily Lesson Planning

PACING

Some students will begin the process of learning to read slowly but make rapid progress later. To be at grade level by the end of the year, first graders need to complete Unit 20 by the end of the 18th week of school. Groups that are working at a slower pace may require more intensive *Read Well* instruction and practice. (See *Getting Started: A Guide to Implementation.*)

A BASIC RULE (Reminder)
Make adjustments frequently, moving students as quickly as possible without sacrificing mastery.

ASSESSMENT

Upon completion of this unit, assess each student and proceed to Unit 14 as appropriate.

SAMPLE LESSON PLANS

The sample lesson plans illustrate how materials can be used for students with different learning needs. Each lesson plan is designed to provide daily decoding practice and story reading.

Note: Students who typically complete a unit in two days should follow the 3-Day Plan for this unit. The slower pace will allow students to master both /rrr/ as in "rabbit" and the new spelling pattern /ea/.

3-DAY PLAN		
Day 1	**Day 2**	**Day 3**
• Decoding Practice 1	• Decoding Practice 2	• Decoding Practice 3
• Stories 1 and 2	• Stories 3 and 4	• Stories 5 and 6 and Story Summary
• Skill Work 1*	• Skill Work 3*	• Skill Work 5*
• Comprehension Work 2*	• Comprehension Work 4*	• Skill Work 6*
• Homework 1, Story 2*	• Homework 2, Story 4*	• Homework 3, Story 6*
		• Homework 4, Storybook Decoding Review*

4-DAY PLAN			
Day 1	**Day 2**	**Day 3**	**Day 4**
• Decoding Practice 1	• Decoding Practice 2	• Decoding Practice 3	• Decoding Practice 4
• Stories 1 and 2	• Stories 3 and 4	• Stories 5 and 6 and Story Summary	• Review Stories 2, 4, and 6
• Skill Work 1*	• Skill Work 3*	• Skill Work 5*	• Skill Work 6*
• Comprehension Work 2*	• Comprehension Work 4*	• Homework 3, Story 6*	• Homework 4, Storybook Decoding Review*
• Homework 1, Story 2*	• Homework 2, Story 4*		

* From *Read Well* Comprehension and Skill Work (workbook), *Read Well* Homework (blackline masters), or Extra Practice in this book.

6-DAY PLAN • *Pre-Intervention*

Day 1	**Day 2**	**Day 3**
• Decoding Practice 1 • Story 1 • Skill Work 1*	• Review Decoding Practice 1 • Story 2 • Comprehension Work 2* • Homework 1, Story 2*	• Decoding Practice 2 • Story 3 • Skill Work 3*
Day 4	**Day 5**	**Day 6**
• Review Decoding Practice 2 • Story 4 • Comprehension Work 4* • Homework 2, Story 1*	• Decoding Practice 3 • Story 5 • Skill Work 5* • Homework 4, Storybook Decoding Review*	• Decoding Practice 4 • Story 6 and Story Summary • Skill Work 6* • Homework 3, Story 6*

PRE-INTERVENTION AND INTERVENTION

See *Getting Started: A Guide to Implementation* for information on how to achieve mastery at a faster pace with students who require six or more days of instruction.

8-DAY PLAN • *Intervention*

Day 1	**Day 2**	**Day 3**	**Day 4**
• Decoding Practice 1 • Story 1 • Skill Work 1*	• Review Decoding Practice 1 • Story 2 • Comprehension Work 2* • Homework 1, Story 2*	• Decoding Practice 2 • Story 3 • Skill Work 3*	• Review Decoding Practice 2 • Story 4 • Comprehension Work 4* • Homework 2, Story 4*
Day 5	**Day 6**	**Day 7**	**Day 8**
• Decoding Practice 3 • Story 5 • Skill Work 5* • Homework 4, Storybook Decoding Review*	• Decoding Practice 4 • Story 6 and Story Summary • Skill Work 6* • Homework 3, Story 6*	• Extra Practice 1* • Extra Practice Activity 1*	• Extra Practice 2* • Extra Practice Activity 2*

10-DAY PLAN • *Intervention*

Day 1	**Day 2**	**Day 3**	**Day 4**	**Day 5**
• Decoding Practice 1 • Story 1 • Skill Work 1*	• Review Decoding Practice 1 • Story 2 • Comprehension Work 2* • Homework 1, Story 2*	• Decoding Practice 2 • Story 3 • Skill Work 3*	• Review Decoding Practice 2 • Story 4 • Comprehension Work 4* • Homework 2, Story 4*	• Decoding Practice 3 • Story 5 • Skill Work 5* • Homework 4, Storybook Decoding Review*
Day 6	**Day 7**	**Day 8**	**Day 9**	**Day 10**
• Decoding Practice 4 • Story 6 and Story Summary • Skill Work 6* • Homework 3, Story 6*	• Extra Practice 1* • Extra Practice Activity 1*	• Extra Practice 2* • Extra Practice Activity 2*	• Extra Practice 3 • Storybook Decoding Review • Review Solos: Units 10 and 11** • Extra Practice Activity 3*	• Extra Practice 4 • Review Decoding Practice 4 • Review Solos: Units 12 and 13** • Extra Practice Activity 4*

** Use review stories as listed or substitute with stories from *Read Well* K, Unit 13

Materials and Materials Preparation

 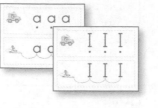

Core Lessons

Teacher Materials

READ WELL **MATERIALS**

- Unit 13 Teacher's Guide
- Sound and Word Cards for Units 1–13
- Smooth and Bumpy Blending Cards 24, 25, 26, 27
- Spring toys (optional for use with Stretch and Shrink)
- Game markers (optional for use with cover-up activities)
- *Assessment Manual* or page 56

SCHOOL SUPPLIES

- Stopwatch or watch with a second hand

Student Materials

READ WELL **MATERIALS**

- Decoding Book 2 for each student
- Unit 13 Storybook for each student
- Unit 13 Comprehension and Skill Work for each student
  (My Activity Book 2)
- Unit 13 Certificate of Achievement (blackline master page 57)
- Unit 13 Homework for each student (blackline masters)
  See *Getting Started* for suggested homework routines.

SCHOOL SUPPLIES

- Pencils, colors (optional—markers, crayons, or colored pencils)

Make one copy per student of each blackline master as appropriate for the group.

Note: For new or difficult Comprehension and Skill Work activities, make overhead transparencies from the blackline masters. Use the transparencies to demonstrate and guide practice.

Extra Practice Lessons

Note: Use these lessons only if needed.

Student Materials

READ WELL **MATERIALS**

- Unit 13 Extra Practice 1 and 2 for each student (blackline master pages 59 and 63)
- Unit 13 Extra Practice Activities 1, 2, 3, and 4 for each student (blackline master pages 60-61 double-sided; 64; 66–67 single-sided; 68)

SCHOOL SUPPLIES

- Pencils, colors (markers, crayons, or colored pencils), highlighters, scissors, glue
- White boards or paper

Important Tips

In this section, you will find:

★ Onset and Rime With "At"

Word families are practiced in *Read Well* to help children take advantage of the common patterns found in English. Once children understand the patterned nature of letter combinations, some children are able to induce new patterns on their own.

★ Diagnostic-Prescriptive Teaching

The role of the teacher in bringing all children to mastery is essential to the success of high-risk readers. Review critical principles in diagnostic-prescriptive teaching.

★ Language Priming—Using "With"

Use the information on page 10 to encourage English Language Learners and children with language delays to use the language patterns provided in *Read Well*. Continuous use of the same patterns will help children master the basics. The sample lesson provides a model for how to practice using the word "with."

★ Onset and Rime With "At"

ONSETS AND RIMES

Rimes are the common letter patterns found in rhyming words. Onsets are the consonants that precede the rime. Use Blending Card 26 to review recognition of rimes, with the new sound /rrr/.

BLENDING CARD 26

- Have students do Smooth Blending of *at*.
  Do Smooth Blending of the first small word.
  Loop under each letter. (/aaat/)
  Say the word. (at)
  Use the word in a sentence.
  Where are we? (At [school])

- Have students read the underline part of *rat*, and then read the whole word.
  Read the small word. (at)
  Read the whole word. (rat)
  Use the word in a sentence.
  What rhymes with *rat*? ([hat])

- Have students read the underline part of *cat*, and then read the whole word.
  Read the small word. (at)
  Read the whole word. (cat)
  Use the word in a sentence.
  What does a *cat* say? (A *cat* says "meow.")

- Have students read all three words.
  Read the whole list.
  First word. (at)
  Next. (rat)
  Next. (cat)

- Repeat practice. Mix group and individual turns, independent of your voice. Point to the words in random order. Build fluency with each repetition.

Research Snapshot

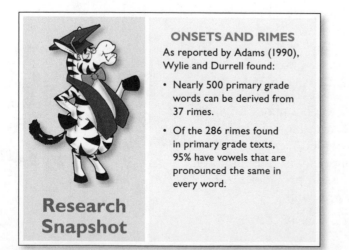

Research Snapshot

ONSETS AND RIMES
As reported by Adams (1990), Wylie and Durrell found:

- Nearly 500 primary grade words can be derived from 37 rimes.

- Of the 286 rimes found in primary grade texts, 95% have vowels that are pronounced the same in every word.

★Diagnostic-Prescriptive Teaching

Adopting a research-based program is no guarantee that all children will learn. Some children learn to read with ease, while others find learning to read as unnatural as solving quadratic equations. For these children, diagnostic-prescriptive teaching is critical. The principles below will help you bring all children to full literacy.

1 ADHERE TO ASSESSMENT GUIDELINES.

Passing students along with kindness is a guarantee for later failure. Use the assessments to determine what students know and need to learn. Provide Jell-Well Reviews as needed.

2 DURING LESSONS USE MASTERY-BASED TEACHING PROCEDURES.

If children master each unit before proceeding to the next unit, gentle diagnostic corrections within units create success. Keep in mind the important steps to mastery. Then, provide practice as needed on the skills and words presented.

Word Reading Errors
- During Decoding Practice, write any missed word on a white board or paper.
- During Story Reading, write any missed word on a white board or paper and practice the words between readings.

  Example: Students read "Tam" when the word is "Tad."
  Have students identify the incorrect sound.
  Point to the incorrect sound. Tell me the sound. (/d/)
  Have students blend the word again with the correct sound.
  Sound it out. (/Taaaad/)
  Say the word. (Tad)

- Practice other words.
- Return to the difficult word at least three times.
- Acknowledge student responses.

Comprehension
Adhere to the questions and Teacher Think Alouds presented in the Teacher's Guide. If students have difficulty with a comprehension question, think aloud with them or reread the portion of the story that answers the question. Then, ask the question again.

3 PROVIDE REPEATED READINGS.

Read Well student-read text is carefully designed to include only words that can be sounded out based on known skills. Materials that do not correlate with *Read Well* can create confusion and overload for a high-risk reader—requiring students to engage in frustrating guessing.

Have students do repeated readings with Solo Stories, Homework, and Extra Practice. You may wish to borrow *Read Well* K storybooks to expand practice options.

★Language Priming—Using "With"

Continued review and a conscious attention to the language patterns in *Read Well* can augment a more formal language intervention. Review the sample lessons provided in Units 2–10 on a regular basis. The lesson below provides a sample for how to practice using "with" in oral and written language.

◆◆ FOR ENGLISH LANGUAGE LEARNERS AND CHILDREN WITH LANGUAGE DELAYS

EXAMPLE: **Students are introduced to the question/response pattern in Unit 12: Who do you go to school *with*? (I go to school *with* my friends.)**

MATERIALS: Make cards out of heavy paper.
Written words: with the Miss Tam cat is The
Picture words: {dog} {classmates' photos}

NEW PROCEDURE

Show students a picture from the Unit 12 storybook showing Miss Tam and the cat. Say something like:
Who is in the picture? (Miss Tam)
Who is *with* Miss Tam? (The cat is *with* Miss Tam.)
Help students make the written sentence using the cards.
Repeat with other pictures, decodable words, and picture words.

ORAL LANGUAGE PATTERNS	
Introduced in This Unit and Reviewed From Previous Units	
★ What do you like to *read*? (I like to *read* [my book].)	★ [Mr. Z] gave us [cookies]. He gave us … (*sweets*).
★ Something good to eat is a … (*treat*).	★ [Michael] is *near* the [door]. Where is [Michael]?
★ What rhymes with "*rat*"? ([Cat])	★ When people laugh, they say … ("*Tee hee*").
★ When I'm hungry, I need to … (*eat*).	★ I *want* a [snack].
★ What does a tiger eat? (*Meat*)	★ [Jessica] *wants* a [dog].
★ It's time for [reading]. Please take your … (*seat*).	An animal with antlers is a *deer*.
★ The children *ran* a race.	The bear is up in the … (*tree*).
★ Some people say "*Rats!*" when something is wrong.	The dog *hid* under the bed.
★ *Tad* is a boy's name. Are you *Tad*? ([No])	This apple tastes good. It is *sweet* and juicy.
★ *Can* you [read]? (Yes, I can.)	Where are we? (At school)
★ *Three* children are [reading]. How many are [reading]? (Three)	What does a *cat* say? (A *cat* says "meow.")
★ If you have a question, raise your … (*hand*).	What does a mad cat do? (*Hiss*)
★ [Mary] got [poison oak] so [she] had a … (*rash*).	The *wind* is blowing the [leaves].
★ Another word for garbage is … (*trash*).	What is this? (This is *an* [apple].)
★ If you keep your desk clean, you are … (*neat*).	What *can* we do? (We *can* [read].)
★ Today I will swim; yesterday I … (*swam*).	What is *this*? (*This* is a [pencil].)
★ The [bear] ate three … (*hams*).	What do you do in a swimming pool? (*Swim*)

How to Teach the Lessons

★ Stars signal new skills, activities, or stories. ★

Teach from this section. Each instructional component is outlined in an easy-to-teach format. Special tips are provided to help you nurture student progress.

In this section, you will find:

Decoding Practice 1
- Unit Introduction
- Story 1, Duet
- Skill Work Activity 1
- Story 2, Solo
- Comprehension Work Activity 2

Decoding Practice 2
- Story 3, Duet
- Skill Work Activity 3
- Story 4, Solo
- Comprehension Work Activity 4

Decoding Practice 3
- Story 5, Duet
- Skill Work Activity 5
- Story 6, Solo
- Story Summary
- Skill Work Activity 6

Decoding Practice 4
Review Solo Stories

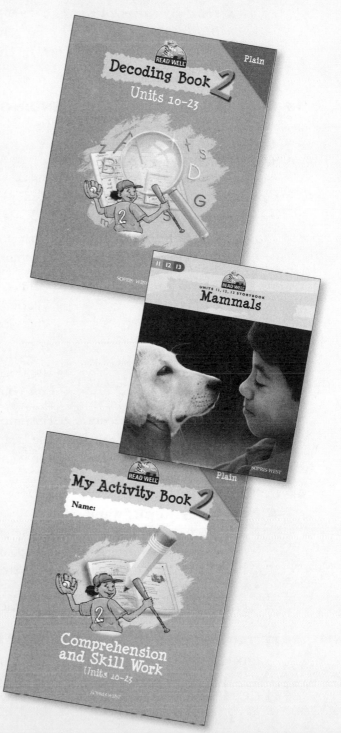

SCAFFOLDED INSTRUCTION
Developmental Shift (Important Reminder)

As children gain confidence across units, begin with guided practice or independent practice, as appropriate.

If a new word is difficult, you may wish to begin with a demonstration and guided practice.

① SOUND REVIEW

② NEW SOUND INTRODUCTION

<u>R</u> can be hard because students often say /er/ instead of /rrr/. Have them say "roar," then stop them after the first /rrr/. Say something like: That's the /rrr/ we need to hear.

③ NEW SOUND PRACTICE

◆◆ **④ STRETCH AND SHRINK**

read-rrreaeaead-read	What do you like to *read*? (I like to *read* [my book].)
hid-hiiid-hid	The dog *hid* under the bed.
sweet-ssswwweeeet-sweet	This apple tastes good. It is *sweet* and juicy.
treat-trrreaeaeat-treat	Something good to eat is a . . . (*treat*).

◆◆ **⑤ SMOOTH AND BUMPY BLENDING—CARDS 26, 27**

◆◆ **⑥ SOUNDING OUT SMOOTHLY**

★ **New blends: /tr-/ and /Thr-/**

Have students say the underlined part, sound out the word, and then read the word. Use the words in sentences as needed.

✿	*rrraaannn-ran*	The children *ran* a race.
	Rrraaatsss-Rats	Some people say "*Rats!*" when something is wrong.
	deeeerrr-deer	An animal with antlers is a *deer*.
♥	*Taaad-Tad*	*Tad* is a boy's name. Are you *Tad*? ([No])
	Hiiissss-Hiss	What does a mad cat do? (*Hiss*)
	caaat-cat	What does a *cat* say? (A *cat* says "meow.")
☆	*raaat-rat*	What rhymes with "*rat*"? ([Cat])
	hiiid-hid	The dog *hid* under the bed.
	Caaannn-Can	*Can* you [read]? (Yes, I *can*.)
●	*ssswwweeeet-sweet*	This apple tastes good. It is *sweet* and juicy.
	trrreeee-tree	The bear is up in the . . . (*tree*).
	Thththrrreeee-Three	*Three* children are [reading]. How many are [reading]?

◆◆ **⑦ TRICKY WORDS**

★ **New Tricky Word: "want"**

• Introduce the new word "want." Say something like:

If I sounded out your new word, it would sound like this /wwwăăănnnt/. I don't say, "I /wănt/ a snack." I say, "want." "I want a snack." Say your new word three times. (Want, want, want)

• Have students use "want" in sentences.

• Repeat the row. Mix group and individual turns, independent of your voice.

⑧ DAILY STORY READING

Proceed to the Unit 13 Storybook. See Daily Lesson Planning for pacing suggestions.

⑨ COMPREHENSION AND SKILL WORK ACTIVITY I AND/OR ACTIVITY 2

See pages 21 and/or 25.

UNIT 13 DECODING PRACTICE I
(For use with Stories 1 and 2)

1. SOUND REVIEW Use Sound Cards for Units 1–12.

2. NEW SOUND INTRODUCTION Have students echo (repeat) the phrases. Do not have students read the poem.

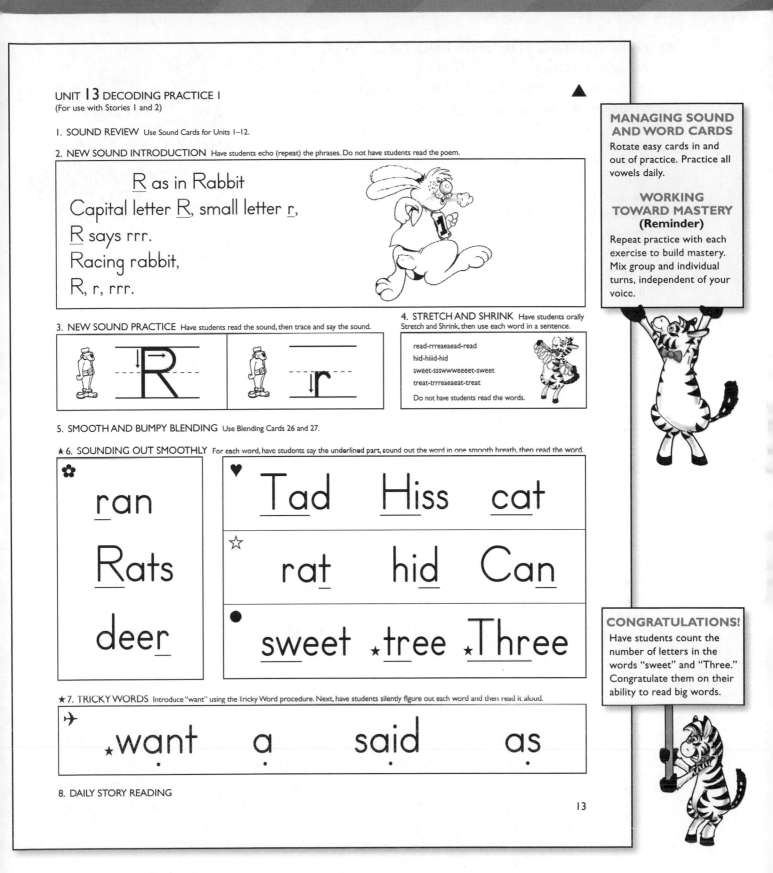

R as in Rabbit
Capital letter R, small letter r,
R says rrr.
Racing rabbit,
R, r, rrr.

3. NEW SOUND PRACTICE Have students read the sound, then trace and say the sound.

R   r

4. STRETCH AND SHRINK Have students orally Stretch and Shrink, then use each word in a sentence.

read-rrreaeaead-read
hid-hiiid-hid
sweet-ssswwweeeet-sweet
treat-trrreaeaeat-treat

Do not have students read the words.

5. SMOOTH AND BUMPY BLENDING Use Blending Cards 26 and 27.

★ 6. SOUNDING OUT SMOOTHLY For each word, have students say the underlined part, sound out the word in one smooth breath, then read the word.

❀
ran
Rats
deer

♥
Tad   Hiss   cat

☆
rat   hid   Can

●
sweet   ★tree   ★Three

★ 7. TRICKY WORDS Introduce "want" using the Tricky Word procedure. Next, have students silently figure out each word and then read it aloud.

✈
★want   a   said   as

8. DAILY STORY READING

13

1 INTRODUCING THE UNIT AND TITLE PAGE

Identifying—Title

Tell students the title of the Unit is "Mammals in Winter."

Priming Background Knowledge

Look at the first picture. What mammal do you think the first story is about? (A rabbit)

Look at the next picture. What mammal do you think the next story is about? (A bear)

Teacher Think Aloud

The Unit is called "Mammals in Winter." I wonder if we will find out new facts about rabbits and bears in the winter.

2 INTRODUCING VOCABULARY

Vocabulary—Rabbit, Bear, Rat

Rabbit

Put your finger under the first picture.

A *rabbit* is a mammal that hops and eats carrots.

Bear

Put your finger under the next picture.

A *bear* is a mammal with thick fur and sharp claws.

Rat

Put your finger under the next picture.

That's a picture of a rat.

A *rat* is a mammal that looks like a big mouse.

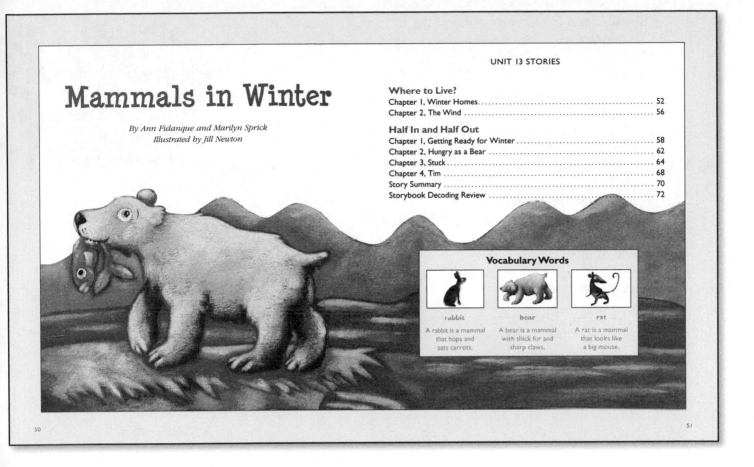

Mammals in Winter

By Ann Fidanque and Marilyn Sprick
Illustrated by Jill Newton

UNIT 13 STORIES

Where to Live?

Half In and Half Out

Vocabulary Words

rabbit	bear	rat
A rabbit is a mammal that hops and eats carrots.	A bear is a mammal with thick fur and sharp claws.	A rat is a mammal that looks like a big mouse.

50   51

Vocabulary Words

rabbit	bear	rat
A rabbit is a mammal that hops and eats carrots.	A bear is a mammal with thick fur and sharp claws.	A rat is a mammal that looks like a big mouse.

Defining Vocabulary—Rabbit, Bear, Rat

DUET STORY READING INSTRUCTIONS

Students read from their own storybooks.
The teacher reads the small text and students read the large text.

PACING

- 3- to 4-Day Plans: Have students do the first reading of Duet Story 1.
  Then proceed to repeated readings of Solo Story 2.
- 6- to 10-Day Plans: Have students do the first *and* second readings.

COMPREHENSION BUILDING:
DISCUSSION QUESTIONS AND TEACHER THINK ALOUDS

Ask questions and discuss text on the first or second reading when indicated in the storybook in light gray text.

PROCEDURES

1. First Reading

Have students choral read the student text.

2. Second Reading

Have students take turns, with each student reading one line of student text.

Where to Live?

CHAPTER 1
Winter Homes

Tad was a sweet wild rabbit.
What kind of animal was Tad?[1] (A rabbit)

He was born in the spring.
What season was Tad born in?[2] (In the spring)

He had lived and played in the fields all summer and fall.

52

❶ Identifying—What

❷ Identifying—What

**FINGER TRACKING
(Reminder)**
Continue having children track
the large text with their fingers.

Now winter was coming.

<u>The</u> <u>wind</u> <u>was</u> getting cold.

<u>The</u> <u>rats</u> <u>and the</u> squirrels had built nests.

<u>Three</u> <u>deer</u> <u>had</u> moved down the mountain.

<u>Tad</u> <u>said,</u> <u>"I</u> <u>need a</u> winter home too."

It was getting cold. What season was coming?[1] (Winter)
What did the rats and squirrels do to get ready for winter?[2] (They built nests.)
What is Tad's problem?[3] (He needs a winter home.)

MAKING CONNECTIONS
After completing the page, say something like: It's winter in a cold place, so the animals are getting ready for winter. Close your eyes and imagine that it is snowing. What would you do to stay warm?

53

❶ Identifying—What
❷ Inferring
❸ Identifying—Problem

Note: Questions focus students on important story elements and provide prompts for story discussions. Answers provide guidance, not verbatim responses.

Tad saw a snake slither under a rock. "That looks like a nice winter home," said Tad. So Tad tried to join the snake underneath the rock.

What do you think the snake thought about Tad joining him under the rock?[1]

"Hiss," said the snake. "Go away!"

What did the snake say to Tad?[2] (Go away)

Tad ran as fast as he could.

Then Tad saw a toad who had buried herself in the mud to stay warm.

"Can I sit with you in the mud through the long winter

months?" asked Tad.

What was the toad doing to stay warm in the winter?[3] (She was sitting in the mud.)
Do you think Tad should sit in the mud all winter long?[4]

54

BUILDING COMPREHENSION
Reading and Thinking Aloud (Reminder)
If students have difficulty with a comprehension question, think aloud with them or reread the portion of the story that answers the question. Then, ask the question again.

❶ Inferring
❷ Identifying—What
❸ Explaining
❹ Responding, Inferring

"What?" asked the toad.

"**I** <u>**want**</u> to sit in the mud," said Tad.

"**I** <u>**want a**</u> nice warm place to stay for the cold winter months."

What did Tad want to do?¹(Sit in the mud; find a warm place for winter)

VISUALIZING

After reading the page, say something like:

Look at the picture. Why was the toad sitting in the mud? (To keep warm)

Close your eyes, imagine sitting in the mud. Do you think that would be a good way to keep warm?

TEACHER THINK ALOUD

I think sitting in the mud might be a way to keep warm if you didn't have a jacket or nice warm fur to keep you warm. I think I'd rather have a jacket!

The toad said, "Silly rabbit. You do not want to sit in the mud with me. You have a beautiful fur coat that will keep you warm through the cold winter months. You can still run and play. Rabbits in fur coats don't need a special winter home."

In the end, what did Tad learn?²(He learned that rabbits don't need special winter homes because they have thick fur.)

55

❶ **Identifying**

❷ **Inferring**

SOUND PAGE

Use work pages from the workbook.

CHECKOUT OPPORTUNITY

While students are working on Comprehension and Skill Work, you may wish to listen to individuals read a Decoding Practice or Solo Story. If the student makes an error, gently correct and have the student reread the column, row, or sentence.

PROCEDURES

For each step, demonstrate and guide practice as needed.

1. Handwriting—Basic Instructions

- Have students identify the capital letter <u>R</u> as in "Rabbit."
- Have students trace and write the capital letter <u>R</u>—leaving a finger space between each letter. Repeat with small letter <u>r</u> on the next two rows.

2. Drawing Pictures That Begin With /r/—Basic Instructions

- Have students brainstorm possible items.
  Examples: rat, raindrops, rooster, roller skate, rocks, ruler, rainbow . . .
- Have students fill the box with things that begin with /r/. Students can write the letter <u>r</u>, draw pictures of things that begin with /r/, cut out and paste up pictures of things that begin with /r/, or write words that begin with /r/.

Note: Neat work helps students take pride in their efforts.

SOLO STORY READING INSTRUCTIONS
Students read from their own storybooks.

COMPREHENSION BUILDING:
DISCUSSION QUESTIONS AND TEACHER THINK ALOUDS
Ask questions and discuss text on the first or second reading
when indicated in the storybook in light gray text.

PROCEDURES

1. First Reading
Have students identify the picture words {sun} and {house}, then
choral read the text.

2. Second Reading
- Mix group and individual turns, independent of your voice.
  Have students work toward an accuracy goal of 0–2 errors.
  Quietly keep track of errors made by all students in each group.
- After reading the story, practice any difficult words.
- If the group has not reached the accuracy goal, have the group
  reread the story, mixing group and individual turns.

3. Repeated Readings
a. Timed Readings

- Once the accuracy goal has been achieved, have individual
  students read the page while the other children track the text
  with their fingers and whisper read.
  Time individuals for 30 seconds and encourage each student to
  work for his or her personal best.
- Count the number of words read correctly in 30 seconds (words
  read minus errors).
  Multiply by two to determine words read correctly per minute.
  Record student scores.

Note: Time students who are confident and enjoy the challenge.
Accuracy precedes rate. If a student is unable to read with close to
100% accuracy, do not time the student. The personal goal should
be accuracy. If the student is unable to read with accuracy, watch
assessment results carefully. Evaluate group placement. Consider a
Jell-Well Review.

b. Partner Reading

During students' daily independent work, have them do
Partner Reading.

c. Homework 1

Have students read the story at home. (A reprint of this story
is available on a blackline master in *Read Well* Homework.)

CHAPTER 2
The Wind

What is the title of this chapter?[1] ("The Wind")

The wind said, "Www, w, w."

What did the wind say?[2] (The wind said, "Www, w, w.")

The deer ran.

What did the deer do?[3] (The deer ran.)

He said, "I need the 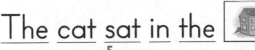 ."

The wind said, "Www, w, w."

Three rats hid in a tree.

What did the three rats do?[4] (The three rats hid in a tree.)

The wind said, "Www, w, w."

The cat sat in the  .

What did the cat do?[5] (The cat sat in the house.)

56

> **FINGER TRACKING**
> **(Reminder)**
> Continue having children track the large text with their fingers.

❶ Identifying—Title
❷ Identifying—What
❸ Identifying—Action
❹ Identifying—Action
❺ Identifying—Action

57

24

SENTENCE COMPREHENSION

Use work pages from the workbook.

Identifying—What, Where

Writing
Identifying—What

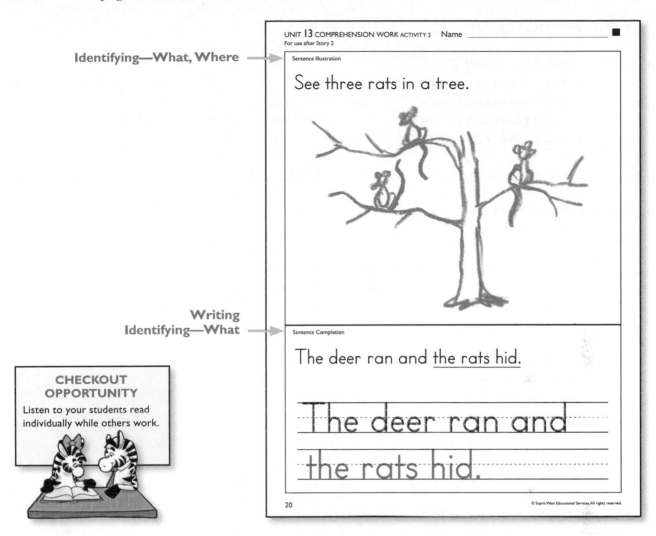

For use after Story 2

Sentence Illustration

See three rats in a tree.

Sentence Completion

The deer ran and the rats hid.

The deer ran and
the rats hid.

20

CHECKOUT OPPORTUNITY

Listen to your students read individually while others work.

PROCEDURES

For each step, demonstrate and guide practice as needed.

1. Sentence Illustration—Basic Instructions

- Have students read the sentence at the top of the page.
- Have students draw a picture of three rats in a tree in the space provided.

2. Sentence Completion—Basic Instructions

- Have students read the complete sentence on the first line.
- Have students read and trace the sentence fragment on the second line.
- Have students copy the end of the sentence on the third line.

Note: You may wish to remind students that a sentence begins with a capital letter and ends with a period.

❶ SOUND REVIEW

Use the Sound Cards for Units 1–13, or the Sound Review on Decoding Practice 4.

❷ BEGINNING SOUND

◆◆ **❸ STRETCH AND SHRINK**

hand-haaannnd-hand	If you have a question, raise your . . . (*hand*).
wind-wwwiiinnnd-wind	The *wind* is blowing the [leaves].
rash-rrraaashshsh-rash	[Mary] got [poison oak] so [she] had a . . . (*rash*).
trash-trrraaashshsh-trash	Another word for garbage is . . . (*trash*).

◆◆ **❹ SMOOTH AND BUMPY BLENDING—CARDS 26, 25**

◆◆ **❺ SOUNDING OUT SMOOTHLY**

★ **New letter combination: ea = ee**

Tell students that <u>ea</u> makes the same sound as <u>ee</u>. Have them practice the Flower Row until they are confident in their recognition of the new spelling for /e/.

- Have students say the underlined part, sound out the word, and then read the word. Use the words in sentences as needed.
- Provide repeated practice, mixing group and individual turns on each word, independent of your voice.

✿ *eaeaeat-eat*	When I'm hungry I need to . . . (*eat*).
mmmeaeaeat-meat	What does a tiger eat? (*Meat*)
nnneaeaeat-neat	If you keep your desk clean, you are . . . (*neat*).
▲ *rrraaannn-ran*	The children *ran* a race.
ssswwwaaammm-swam	Today I will swim; yesterday I . . . (*swam*).
haaammmzzz-hams	The [bear] ate three . . . (*hams*).
ssswwweeeetsss-sweets	[Mr. Z] gave us [cookies]. He gave us . . . (*sweets*).

❻ ACCURACY AND FLUENCY BUILDING

- Have students say, or sound out, the underlined part of the word, then read the word.
- After students have practiced the Heart Column, ask them how "Tim," "him," and "swim" are all the same. (They rhyme. They all end with /-im/.)
- Provide repeated practice. Mix group and individual turns, independent of your voice.

❼ TRICKY WORDS

- Students have had several new Tricky Words. Make sure they can read all of the words with 100% accuracy.
- Provide repeated practice. Mix group and individual turns, independent of your voice.

❽ DAILY STORY READING

Proceed to the Unit 13 Storybook. See Daily Lesson Planning for pacing suggestions.

❾ COMPREHENSION AND SKILL WORK ACTIVITY 3 AND/OR ACTIVITY 4

See pages 33 and/or 37.

Note: The light scripting in *Read Well* will help you visualize instruction as you prepare for a lesson. Scripting provides an instructional guide and is not intended to be memorized or read to students.

◆◆ For ELLs and children with language delays, provide repeated and extended practice with the language patterns. See page 10 for tips.

UNIT 13 DECODING PRACTICE 2
(For use with Stories 3 and 4)

1. SOUND REVIEW Use Sound Cards for Units 1–13 or Sound Review on Decoding Practice 4.

2. BEGINNING SOUND Have students read, trace, and say /rrr/. Next, have students identify both pictures and then point to the one that begins with /rrr/.

3. STRETCH AND SHRINK Have students orally Stretch and Shrink, then use each word in a sentence.

hand-haaannnd-hand
wind-wwwiiinnnd-wind
rash-rrraaashshsh-rash
trash-trrraaashshsh-trash

Do not have students read the words.

4. SMOOTH AND BUMPY BLENDING Use Blending Cards 26 and 25.

★5. SOUNDING OUT SMOOTHLY For each word, have students say the underlined part, sound out the word in one smooth breath, and then read the word.

✿ | ★<u>ea=ee</u> | <u>ea</u>t | m<u>ea</u>t | n<u>ea</u>t
▲ | <u>r</u>an | <u>sw</u>am | <u>h</u>ams | <u>sw</u>eets

6. ACCURACY/FLUENCY BUILDING For each column, have students say the underlined part, then read each word. Next, have students read the column.

♥	☆	✿
T<u>im</u>	h<u>e</u>	Cat
h<u>im</u>	tr<u>ee</u>	<u>can</u>'t
sw<u>im</u>	thr<u>ee</u>	c<u>at</u>s

7. TRICKY WORDS Have students silently figure out each word and then read it aloud.

✈ | a | want | hasn't | The

8. DAILY STORY READING

14

DUET STORY READING INSTRUCTIONS

Students read from their own storybooks.

The teacher reads the small text and students read the large text.

PACING

- 3- to 4-Day Plans: Have students do the first reading of Duet Story 3.

  Then proceed to repeated readings of Solo Story 4.

- 6- to 10-Day Plans: Have students do the first *and* second readings.

COMPREHENSION BUILDING:
DISCUSSION QUESTIONS AND TEACHER THINK ALOUDS

Ask questions and discuss text on the first or second reading when indicated in the storybook in light gray text.

PROCEDURES

1. First Reading

Have students identify the picture word {fish}, then choral read the student text.

2. Second Reading

Have students take turns, with each student reading one line of student text.

Half In and Half Out

CHAPTER I
Getting Ready for Winter

What do you think is going to happen in this story?[1]

Before the long winter comes, bears store fat so they can sleep through the cold winter months. With winter on its way, Tim the bear was hungry—as hungry as a bear!

"Rrr, rrr, rrr," growled Tim.

"I want that meat."

Tim ran and ran for his lunch but the mouse ran faster.

Who is the story about?[2] (Tim the bear)
What did Tim say he wanted to eat?[3] (Meat, the mouse)

MAKING CONNECTIONS
After reading the page, say something like: Look at the mouse. Imagine that you are the little mouse. How would you feel if a big old bear was chasing you?

58

❶ **Predicting**
❷ **Identifying—Who**
❸ **Identifying—What**

"Rrr, rrr, rrr," growled Tim.

"I can eat a ."

What did Tim say he could eat?[1] (A fish)

Tim swam and swam for his lunch.

He caught a large fish, but Tim was still very hungry—as hungry as a bear!

How hungry was Tim after he ate the fish?[2] (Very hungry, as hungry as a bear)

59

❶ Identifying—What

❷ Explaining

Then Tim saw a beehive in a tree on a far-off hill.
What did Tim see in the tree on the hill?[1] (A beehive)

Tim <u>ran</u> <u>and</u> <u>ran</u>.

"<u>Rrr</u>, <u>rrr</u>, <u>rrr</u>," growled Tim.

"<u>I</u> <u>see</u> <u>sweets</u> <u>in</u> <u>that</u> <u>tree</u>," said Tim.

"<u>I</u> <u>can</u> <u>eat</u> <u>sweets</u>!"

Tim climbed the tree and helped himself to the honey. Tim grew fatter and fatter, but Tim was still hungry—as hungry as a bear!
How hungry was Tim after he ate the honey?[2] (As hungry as a bear)

FOCUS ON EXPRESSION

After reading the page, say something like:

Who's talking on this page? (Tim)
I think Tim would have a big, deep, growly voice. Let's read the page again, beginning with "Tim ran." When we read what Tim says, let's use a big, growly voice.
After reading in growly voices, acknowledge their efforts.
[Nick] sounded just like a bear!

60

❶ **Identifying—What**

❷ **Explaining**

61

ALPHABET DETECTIVE

Use work pages from the workbook.

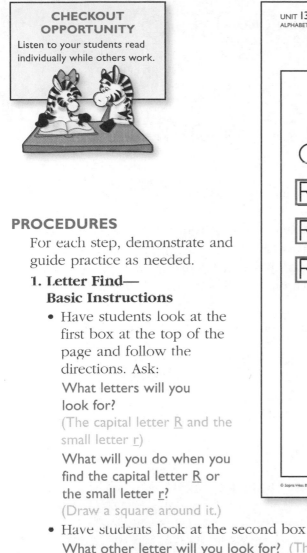

CHECKOUT OPPORTUNITY

Listen to your students read individually while others work.

PROCEDURES

For each step, demonstrate and guide practice as needed.

1. Letter Find—Basic Instructions

- Have students look at the first box at the top of the page and follow the directions. Ask:

  What letters will you look for?

  (The capital letter R and the small letter r)

  What will you do when you find the capital letter R or the small letter r?

  (Draw a square around it.)

UNIT 13 SKILL WORK ACTIVITY 3   Name _____

ALPHABET DETECTIVE: For use after Story 3

R r   t

R as in Rabbit

Capital letter R, small letter r.

R says rrr.

Racing rabbit

R, r, rrr.

  21

- Have students look at the second box at the top of the page. Ask:

  What other letter will you look for? (The small letter t)

  What will you do when you find the small letter t? (Draw a circle around it.)

- Tell students to follow the directions in the first box for the whole poem; then follow the directions in the second box for the whole poem.

2. Self-Monitoring—Basic Instructions

Have students systematically check each line after finishing the task.

Alternative: At the beginning of the exercise, tell students the number of R's they will draw a square around, and the number of t's they will circle. Have students write the numbers on the top of their paper. When students complete the activity, have them count the number of circles and squares they have drawn. If the numbers are incorrect, they can recheck each line.

3. Coloring—Optional

Have students carefully color the picture, using at least three colors.

Note: If students have difficulty with the multi-step directions, have them do just the first step.

SOLO STORY READING INSTRUCTIONS
Students read from their own storybooks.

COMPREHENSION BUILDING:
DISCUSSION QUESTIONS AND TEACHER THINK ALOUDS
Ask questions and discuss text on the first or second reading
when indicated in the storybook in light gray text.

PROCEDURES

1. First Reading
Have students identify the picture word {bear}, then choral read the text.

2. Second Reading
- Mix group and individual turns, independent of your voice.
  Have students work toward an accuracy goal of 0–2 errors.
  Quietly keep track of errors made by all students in each group.
- After reading the story, practice any difficult words.
- If the group has not reached the accuracy goal, have the group
  reread the story, mixing group and individual turns.

3. Repeated Readings
a. Timed Readings

- Once the accuracy goal has been achieved, have individual
  students read the page while the other children track the text
  with their fingers and whisper read.
  Time individuals for 30 seconds and encourage each student to
  work for his or her personal best.
- Count the number of words read correctly in 30 seconds (words
  read minus errors).
  Multiply by two to determine words read correctly per minute.
  Record student scores.

b. Partner Reading

During students' daily independent work, have them do
Partner Reading.

c. Homework 2

Have students read the story at home. (A reprint of this story
is available on a blackline master in *Read Well* Homework.)

CHAPTER 2
Hungry as a Bear

<u>The</u> <u>man</u> <u>said</u>, "<u>I</u> <u>can</u> <u>see</u> <u>a</u> [bear]."

<u>The</u> <u>man</u> <u>ran</u> <u>and</u> <u>hid</u>.

What did the man see?[1] (A bear)
What did the man do?[2] (He ran and hid.)

<u>Tim</u> <u>said</u>, "<u>I</u> <u>want</u> <u>meat</u>!

<u>I</u> <u>see</u> <u>three</u> <u>hams</u>.

<u>The</u> <u>ham</u> <u>is</u> <u>near</u> <u>that</u> <u>tree</u>.

<u>I</u> <u>can</u> <u>eat</u>, <u>eat</u>, <u>eat</u>.

<u>Mmm</u>, <u>mmm</u>, <u>mmm</u>."

What did Tim want?[3] (Meat)
What did Tim see?[4] (Three hams)
What do you think Tim will do with the hams?[5] (He will eat them.)

62

❶ **Identifying—What**
❷ **Identifying—Action**
❸ **Identifying—Goal**
❹ **Identifying—What**
❺ **Predicting**

FOCUS ON EXPRESSION

After students complete the first reading and before the second reading, have students practice two or three sentences at a time. Demonstrate expressive reading, then give individual turns.

63

36

SENTENCE ILLUSTRATION

Use work pages from the workbook.

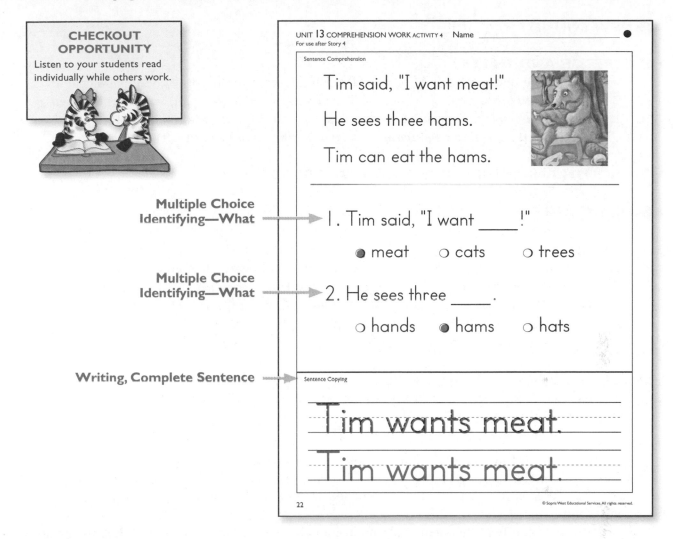

CHECKOUT OPPORTUNITY
Listen to your students read individually while others work.

Multiple Choice Identifying—What

Multiple Choice Identifying—What

Writing, Complete Sentence

UNIT 13 COMPREHENSION WORK ACTIVITY 4   Name _____
For use after Story 4

Sentence Comprehension

Tim said, "I want meat!"

He sees three hams.

Tim can eat the hams.

1. Tim said, "I want _____!"

    ● meat   ○ cats   ○ trees

2. He sees three _____.

    ○ hands   ● hams   ○ hats

Sentence Copying

Tim wants meat.

Tim wants meat.

22   © Sopris West Educational Services. All rights reserved.

PROCEDURES

For each step, demonstrate and guide practice as needed.

1. Sentence Comprehension—Basic Instructions
- Have students read the sentences at the top of the page.
- Have students read items 1 and 2, using the word "blank" when they see the line.
- Have students fill in the circle next to the correct word to fill in the blank.

2. Sentence Tracing and Copying—Basic Instructions
- Have students read the sentence on the first line.
- Have students trace the sentence and copy the sentence.

Note: Remind students that a sentence begins with a capital letter and ends with a period.

① SOUND REVIEW

Use Sound Cards for Units 1–13 or the Sound Review on Decoding Practice 4.

② NEW SOUND PRACTICE

◆◆ ③ STRETCH AND SHRINK

near-nnneaeaearrr-near	[Michael] is *near* the [door]. Where is [Michael]?
neat-nnneaeaeat-neat	If you keep your desk clean, you are . . . (*neat*).
swim-ssswwwiiimmm-swim	What do you do in a swimming pool? (*Swim*)
swam-ssswwwaaammm-swam	Today I will swim; yesterday I . . . (*swam*).

◆◆ ④ SMOOTH AND BUMPY BLENDING—CARDS 27, 24

◆◆ ⑤ SOUNDING OUT SMOOTHLY

- Have students say the underlined part, sound out the word, and then read the word. Use the words in sentences as needed.
- Repeat practice, mixing group and individual turns, independent of your voice.

✿ *Teeee heeee-Tee hee*	When people laugh, they say . . . ("*Tee hee*").
Thththiiisss-This	What is *this*? (*This* is a [pencil].)
Rrraaatsss-Rats	Some people say "*Rats!*" when something is wrong.
Thththrrreeee-Three	*Three* children are [reading]. How many are [reading]?

⑥ ACCURACY AND FLUENCY BUILDING

- For each column, have students say the underlined part, then read each word.
- Have students read the whole column.
- Repeat practice on each column, building accuracy first and then fluency.

Note: The Star and Airplane Columns combine ea and ee words. Ask students what is similar about the words in those columns. (They all rhyme; they end with /ear/ or /eet/.) Ask students which word in each column is spelled with ee. Point out that ee and ea make the same sound.

Once students can read the Heart Column accurately, have them work on building their rate. Have students use the words in pairs of sentences such as, "I can read. I can't fly."

◆◆ ⑦ TRICKY WORDS

★ **New word: "wants"**

- Introduce the new word "wants." Say something like:

  Read the underlined word. (want)

  Now read the whole word. (wants)

  [Jessica] *wants* a [dog].
- Have students read the row.
- Repeat practice on the row. Mix group and individual turns, independent of your voice.

⑧ DAILY STORY READING

Proceed to the Unit 13 Storybook. See Daily Lesson Planning for pacing suggestions.

⑨ COMPREHENSION AND SKILL WORK ACTIVITY 5 AND/OR ACTIVITY 6

See pages 45 and/or 51.

UNIT **13** DECODING PRACTICE 3
(For use with Stories 5 and 6)

1. SOUND REVIEW Use Sound Cards for Units 1–13 or Sound Review on Decoding Practice 4.

2. NEW SOUND PRACTICE Have students read the sound, then trace and say it.

3. STRETCH AND SHRINK Have students orally Stretch and Shrink, then use each word in a sentence.

near-nnneaeaearrr-near
neat-nnneaeaeat-neat
swim-ssswwwiiimmm-swim
swam-ssswwwaaammm-swam

Do not have students read the words.

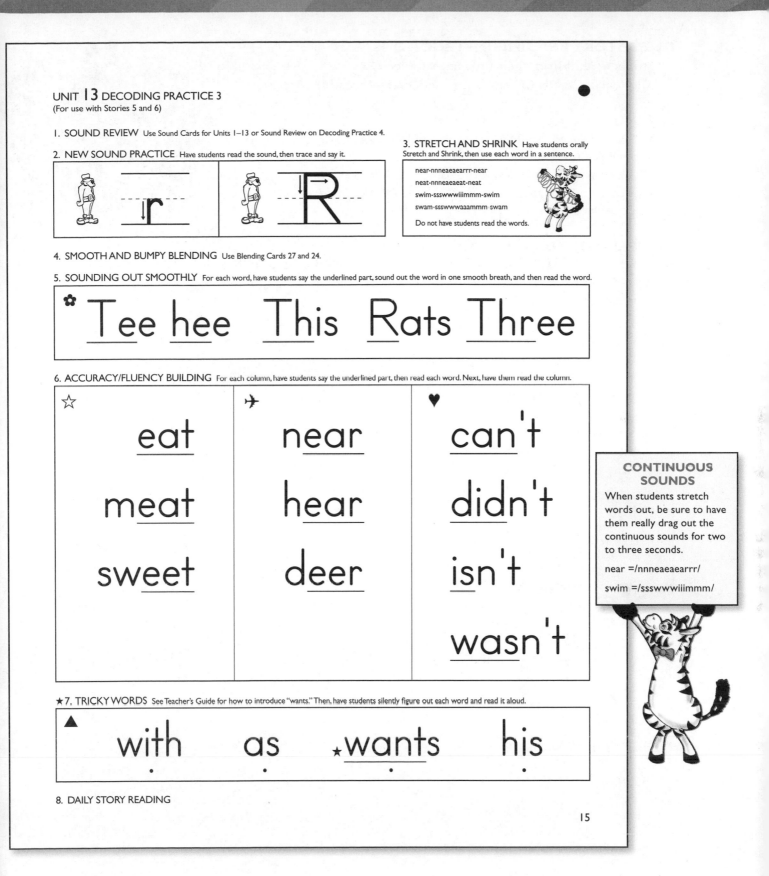

4. SMOOTH AND BUMPY BLENDING Use Blending Cards 27 and 24.

5. SOUNDING OUT SMOOTHLY For each word, have students say the underlined part, sound out the word in one smooth breath, and then read the word.

<u>T</u>ee <u>h</u>ee <u>Th</u>is <u>R</u>ats <u>Th</u>ree

6. ACCURACY/FLUENCY BUILDING For each column, have students say the underlined part, then read each word. Next, have them read the column.

☆

<u>ea</u>t

m<u>ea</u>t

sw<u>ee</u>t

✈

n<u>ea</u>r

h<u>ea</u>r

d<u>ee</u>r

♥

can't

<u>didn't</u>

<u>isn't</u>

<u>wasn't</u>

CONTINUOUS SOUNDS
When students stretch words out, be sure to have them really drag out the continuous sounds for two to three seconds.

near =/nnneaeaearrr/

swim =/ssswwwiiimmm/

★7. TRICKY WORDS See Teacher's Guide for how to introduce "wants." Then, have students silently figure out each word and read it aloud.

▲

with as ★<u>wants</u> his

8. DAILY STORY READING

15

DUET STORY READING INSTRUCTIONS

Students read from their own storybooks.

The teacher reads the small text and students read the large text.

PACING

- 3- to 4-Day Plans: Have students do the first reading
  of Duet Story 5.

  Then proceed to repeated readings of Solo Story 6.
- 6- to 10-Day Plans: Have students do the first *and*
  second readings.

COMPREHENSION BUILDING:
DISCUSSION QUESTIONS AND TEACHER THINK ALOUDS

Ask questions and discuss text on the first or second reading when
indicated in the storybook in light gray text.

PROCEDURES

1. First Reading

- Tell students they are going to read the next chapter about Tim's life.
- Have students choral read the student text.

2. Second Reading

Have students take turns, with each student reading one line of student text.

ECHO READING
(Reminder)

Periodically, repeat the text
with good expression and
phrasing to enhance meaning.

STORY 5, DUET

CHAPTER 3
Stuck

At last, winter came. Snow fell gently on the forest, and Tim was finally satisfied. He had stored huge rolls of fat.
How hungry was Tim when winter finally came? [1] (He wasn't hungry anymore.)

Tim said, "I had meat.

I had sweets. This is the time for me to sleep!"

What did Tim want to do in the winter? [2] (He wanted to sleep.)
Then Tim slowly waddled off to his winter cave. When Tim tried to crawl in his cave, he was in for a surprise!
What do you think the surprise was? [3]

64

① Inferring
② Inferring
③ Predicting

41

Tim said, "I can't get in.

I can't get out."

Poor Tim! He was half in and half out!

He was stuck!

What is Tim's problem? (He was stuck half in and half out of his cave.)

MAKING CONNECTIONS

After completing the page, say something like:

In the last chapters, Tim was really hungry. So, what did he do? (He ate and ate.)
When he ate and ate, he must have gotten . . . (fatter and fatter).
What do you think he is going to do?

❶ Inferring—Problem

STORY 5, DUET

"Tee hee!" said a rat.

"This bear is stuck—half in and half out. I think this cave will make a fine winter home for me."

What did the rat think?[1] (He thought the cave would make a fine home for him.)

Tim didn't say a thing. He just yawned and fell asleep.

What did Tim do?[2] (Tim just yawned and fell asleep.)

The rat ran about busily setting up house.

66

❶ Inferring

❷ Identifying—Action

43

Soon the rat was ready to take a nap.
Just as the rat laid down to rest, Tim began to snore.

"<u>S</u>ss, <u>sss</u>, <u>sss</u>," snored Tim.

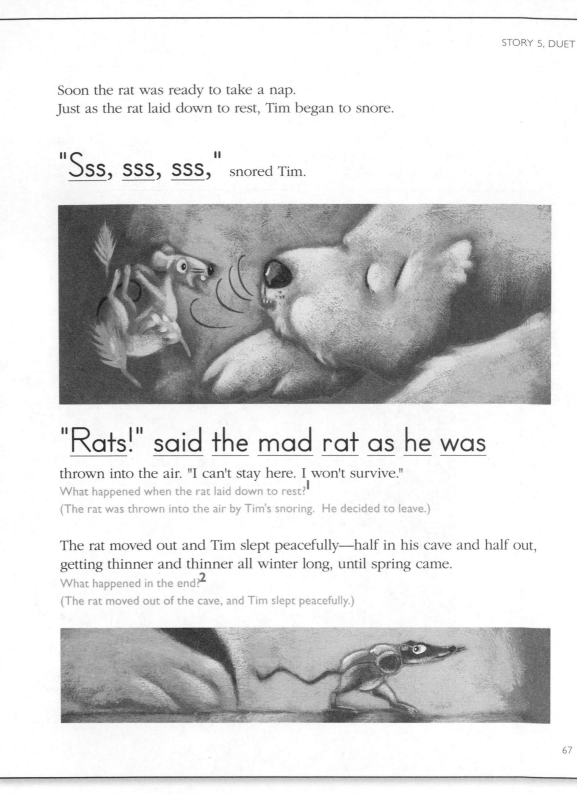

"<u>Rats!</u>" <u>said</u> the <u>mad</u> <u>rat</u> as he <u>was</u>

thrown into the air. "I can't stay here. I won't survive."
What happened when the rat laid down to rest?[1]
(The rat was thrown into the air by Tim's snoring. He decided to leave.)

The rat moved out and Tim slept peacefully—half in his cave and half out,
getting thinner and thinner all winter long, until spring came.
What happened in the end?[2]
(The rat moved out of the cave, and Tim slept peacefully.)

67

❶ Explaining
❷ Explaining—End

HEARING SOUNDS

Use work pages from the workbook.

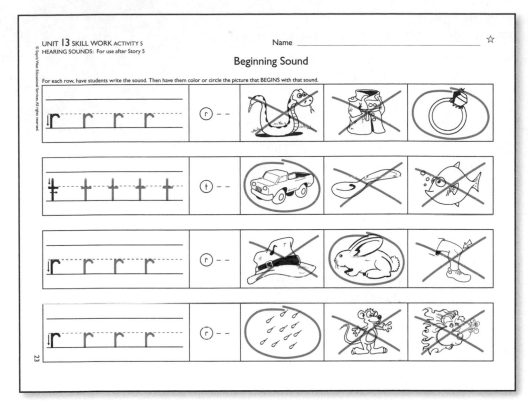

UNIT 13 SKILL WORK ACTIVITY 5
HEARING SOUNDS: For use after Story 5
© Sopris West Educational Services. All rights reserved.

Name _____ ☆

Beginning Sound

For each row, have students write the sound. Then have them color or circle the picture that BEGINS with that sound.

ANSWERS

Line 1: snake, coat, <u>ring</u>
Line 2: <u>truck</u>, spoon, fish
Line 3: hat, <u>rabbit</u>, knee
Line 4: <u>rain</u>, mouse, wind

PROCEDURES

Beginning Sound

Demonstrate and guide practice as needed.

- Have students write the beginning sound on the line.
- Have students color the picture word that begins with that sound.

Alternative: Have students write the beginning sound on the line, circle the picture word that begins with the sound, and cross out the picture words that do not begin with the sound.

PICTURE WORDS
(Reminder)

Make sure that students know which sound they are looking for (beginning) and that they can identify the picture words prior to working independently.

45

SOLO STORY READING INSTRUCTIONS

Students read from their own storybooks.

COMPREHENSION BUILDING:
DISCUSSION QUESTIONS AND TEACHER THINK ALOUDS

Ask questions and discuss text on the first or second reading when indicated in the storybook in light gray text.

PROCEDURES

1. First Reading

Explain to students that their Solo Story is about Tim and the rat.
Have students identify the picture word {sun}, then choral read the text.

2. Second Reading

- Mix group and individual turns, independent of your voice.
  Have students work toward an accuracy goal of 0–2 errors.
  Quietly keep track of errors made by all students in each group.
- After reading the story, practice any difficult words.
- If the group has not reached the accuracy goal, have the group reread the story, mixing group and individual turns.

3. Repeated Readings
a. Timed Readings

- Once the accuracy goal has been achieved, have individual students read the page while the other children track the text with their fingers and whisper read.
  Time individuals for 30 seconds and encourage each student to work for his or her personal best.
- Count the number of words read correctly in 30 seconds (words read minus errors).
  Multiply by two to determine words read correctly per minute. Record student scores.

b. Partner Reading

During students' daily independent work, have them do Partner Reading.

c. Homework 3

Have students read the story at home. (A reprint of this story is available on a blackline master in *Read Well* Homework.)

STORY 6, SOLO

CHAPTER 4

Tim

What is the title of this chapter?[1] ("Tim")

Tim said, "I see the ☐.

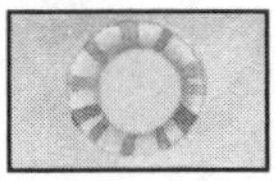

I can eat. I want meat."

Who is the story about?[2] (Tim, the bear)
What did Tim want to do when the sun was warm again?[3] (He wanted to eat meat.)

The rat said, "Tim wants meat.

Rats! I am meat."

See that rat. He ran and ran.

The rat ran and hid!

Why did the rat run and hide?[4] (He didn't want Tim to eat him.)

Tim didn't see the rat.

Did Tim see the rat in the end?[5] (No)

68

❶ Identifying—Title
❷ Identifying—Who
❸ Inferring
❹ Inferring
❺ Identifying

MAKING CONNECTIONS

After completing the page, say something like: Look at the picture. It looks like the weather is getting warmer.

Do you think it's still winter? (No)

How can you tell?

ACKNOWLEDGE ACCOMPLISHMENTS

I am very proud of you. You read that whole chapter about Tim the bear without my help. You even used a growly voice for the bear. Pat yourselves on your backs.

69

COMPREHENSION BUILDING: ORAL STORY RETELL

- Have students study the pictures, then ask questions and discuss the pictures as indicated in the storybook in light gray text. The circle, square, and triangle provide visual references for the beginning, middle, and end of the story.

STORY SUMMARY

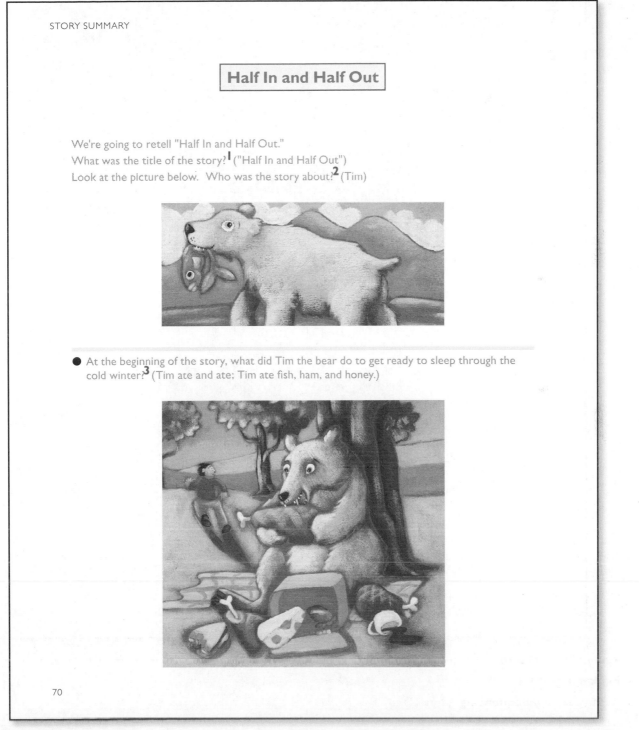

Half In and Half Out

We're going to retell "Half In and Half Out."
What was the title of the story?[1] ("Half In and Half Out")
Look at the picture below. Who was the story about?[2] (Tim)

● At the beginning of the story, what did Tim the bear do to get ready to sleep through the cold winter?[3] (Tim ate and ate; Tim ate fish, ham, and honey.)

70

❶ Identifying—Title

❷ Identifying—Who

❸ Explaining—Beginning

■ In the middle of the story, Tim had stored huge rolls of fat. He was ready to sleep for the winter. What happened to Tim when he tried to crawl in his cave? [1](He was so fat he got stuck.)

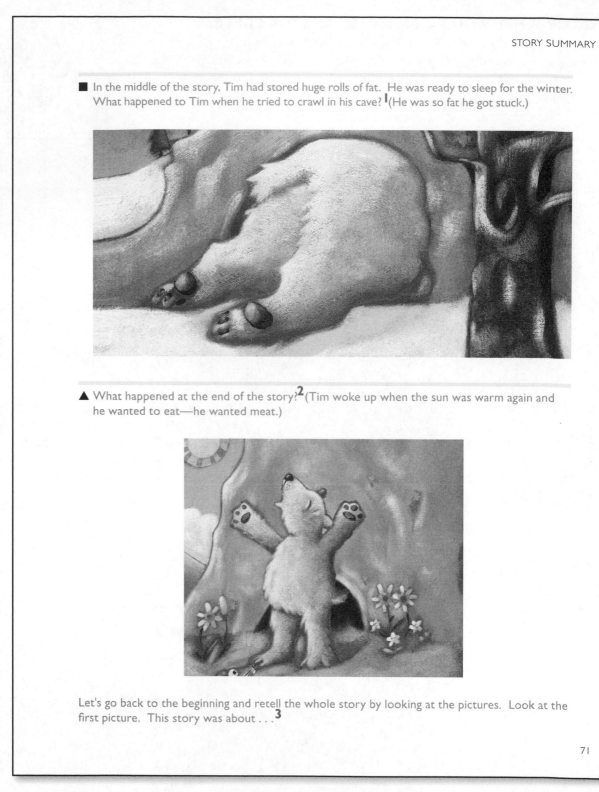

▲ What happened at the end of the story? [2](Tim woke up when the sun was warm again and he wanted to eat—he wanted meat.)

Let's go back to the beginning and retell the whole story by looking at the pictures. Look at the first picture. This story was about . . . [3]

71

❶ Explaining—Middle

❷ Explaining—End

❸ Summarizing, Sequencing

RHYMING PATTERNS

Use work pages from the workbook.

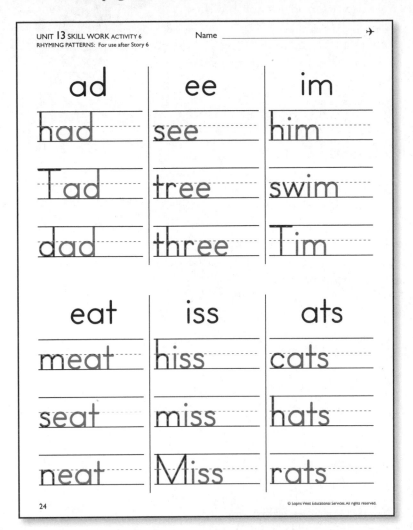

UNIT 13 SKILL WORK ACTIVITY 6
RHYMING PATTERNS: For use after Story 6

Name _____

ad	ee	im
had	see	him
Tad	tree	swim
dad	three	Tim

eat	iss	ats
meat	hiss	cats
seat	miss	hats
neat	Miss	rats

24

CHECKOUT OPPORTUNITY

Listen to your students read individually while others work.

PROCEDURES

Rhyming Patterns—Basic Instructions

- For each box, have students read the pattern at the top and then trace the letters and write the pattern on the lines to make words.
- Remind students to read the pattern words to themselves or to a partner when they finish the exercise.

Note: There are multiple uses for Decoding Practice 4.

- Use the Sound Review rows in place of Sound Card Practice.
- Use the whole page at the end of the unit for fluency building and/or to informally assess skills.
- Have students complete the page as a partner review.
- Build spelling dictation lessons from the sounds and words on this page.

❶ SOUND REVIEW

❷ ACCURACY AND FLUENCY BUILDING
★ Variation

Have fun with the Airplane Columns! Once students have read the column by identifying the underlined part and then reading the word, set a good pace for students. Say something like:

Let's see if you can read the row like this: "meet, sweet, eat, heat, treat."

Then have students read each word three times in a rhythm. Say something like:

Now read each word three times like this: "meet-meet-meet, sweet-sweet-sweet . . ."

❸ TRICKY WORDS

If students seem shaky on the Tricky Words, do not go on to Unit 14. Students should be firm on:

"I," "said," "the," "was," "wasn't," "The," "is," "isn't," "his," "as," "has," "hasn't," "with," "a," and "want."

❹ DAILY STORY READING

See Daily Lesson Planning for story suggestions.

MORE TRICKY WORD PRACTICE

- For independent work times, set up a board game (like Chutes and Ladders) with Tricky Word Cards, and one die. Have students take turns rolling the die and reading the number of cards on the die. Students move one space for each word read correctly. For example, if the student rolls a five, he or she gets to read five Tricky Word Cards and move one space for each word read correctly. The goal is to be the first one to get to the end of the board game.

- Send the list of Tricky Words home for extra practice.

- Provide daily spelling practice with the hardest word. Dictate the word each day. When students can write the word without hesitation, add another word into the daily spelling routine.

UNIT 13 DECODING PRACTICE 4
(See Daily Lesson Planning for story suggestions.)

1. SOUND REVIEW Demonstrate an appropriate pace. Have students read the sounds in each row.

■	C	ea	d	c	h	a	6
❀	t	W	c	i	th	m	12
♥	H	n	ee	w	ea	C	18
●	e	c	s	h	C	i	24

2. ACCURACY/FLUENCY BUILDING For each column, have students say the underlined part, then read each word. Next, have students read the column.

✈	✈✈	✈✈✈	❀	❀❀
m<u>ee</u>t	h<u>id</u>	<u>am</u>	s<u>i</u>t	thr<u>ee</u>
sw<u>ee</u>t	r<u>id</u>	h<u>am</u>	s<u>a</u>t	tr<u>ee</u>
<u>eat</u>	d<u>id</u>	d<u>am</u>	seat	r<u>ea</u>d
h<u>eat</u>	m<u>id</u>	ram	s<u>ee</u>d	rear
tr<u>eat</u>	S<u>id</u>	tr<u>am</u>	s<u>a</u>d	d<u>ee</u>r

RECOGNIZING RIMES

Recognition of the common visual patterns in the words helps facilitate speed of word recognition. The Airplane Columns help students chunk these rimes.

3. TRICKY WORDS Have students silently figure out each word and then read it aloud.

| ☆☆ | want | isn't | a | with | has | 5 |
| ☆☆ | the | his | said | as | wasn't | 10 |

4. DAILY STORY READING

16

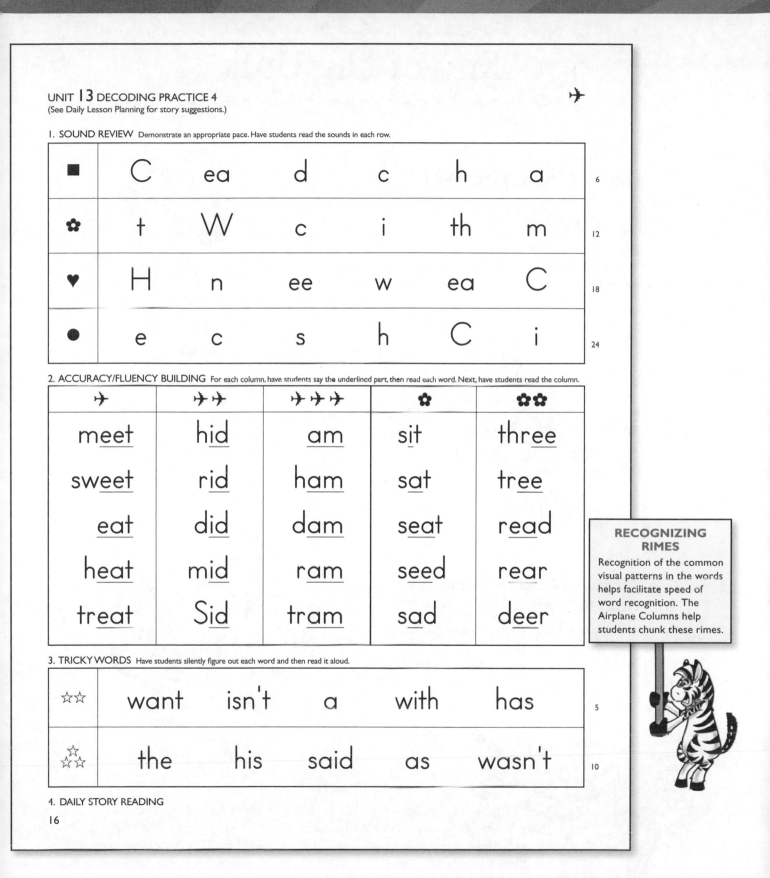

End of the Unit

In this section, you will find:

Making Decisions

As you near the end of the unit, you will need to make decisions. Should you administer the Decoding Assessment or should you teach Extra Practice lessons?

Unit 13 Decoding Assessment

The Unit 13 Decoding Assessment is located on page 56 and can also be found in the *Assessment Manual*.

Certificate of Achievement and Goal Setting

Celebrate your children's accomplishments.

Extra Practice

Lessons and blackline masters for added decoding practice and independent work are provided for students who need extended practice opportunities.

Making Decisions

ASSESSMENT READINESS

Assess when students are able to easily complete decoding tasks from the beginning of a lesson.

- If you aren't sure whether students are ready for the assessment, give the assessment. Do Extra Practice lessons if needed.
- If students are not ready for the assessment, proceed to Extra Practice lessons. Administer the assessment as soon as students are ready.

GENERAL ASSESSMENT GUIDELINES

- Assess each child individually.
- Score student responses on the Student Assessment Record, adhering to the scoring criteria in the *Assessment Manual*. Use a stopwatch to time how long it takes the student to read Subtest D.
- Follow the general instructions at the bottom of each assessment. Record a Strong Pass, a Weak Pass, or a No Pass.

SPECIAL SCORING INFORMATION

Sounding Out Smoothly

If a student reads the word without sounding out in Subtest B, give the student positive feedback, but check to see that the student can sound out the word. Say something like: You can read the word very easily. Now I'd like to see if you can sound it out slowly and smoothly—really stretch that word out.

ACCELERATION

- If students score 100% across all subtests and read Subtest D in less than 30 seconds, consider shortening units. Do not skip Unit 14.
- If an individual student scores 100% across all subtests and reads Subtest D significantly faster than other students in the group, assess the student for placement in the next higher group.

INTERVENTION OPTIONS—INDIVIDUALS

1. Add informal practice throughout the day.
2. Add practice with repeated readings on Solo Stories.
3. Find ways to provide a double dose of *Read Well* instruction.
   - Have the student work in his or her group *and* a lower group.
   - Have an instructional assistant, older student, or parent volunteer preview or review lessons.
   - Have an instructional assistant provide instruction with Extra Practice.
4. Consider placement in a lower group. If one child's fluency scores are significantly lower than the other children in the group, success will be impossible without additional and intensive practice.

INTERVENTION OPTIONS—GROUP

1. Extend the unit with Extra Practice lessons.
2. Consider a Jell-Well Review before moving forward. (See the *Assessment Manual*.)

CERTIFICATE OF ACHIEVEMENT AND GOAL SETTING

When students pass the assessment, celebrate with the Certificate of Achievement. Then, set a personal goal. (See *Getting Started*.)

SUBTEST A. SOUNDS   GOAL 6/7

r   C   a   d   R   ea   h

SUBTEST B. SOUNDING OUT SMOOTHLY   GOAL 4/5

rat   He   dim   can   sweet

SUBTEST C. TRICKY WORDS   GOAL 3/4

is   want   I'm   has

SUBTEST D. SENTENCES Desired Fluency: 30 seconds or less (34 wcpm)   GOAL 15/17

The deer ran in the mist.

Nan meets Sam at the tree.

Tad didn't eat with me.

SCORING	If the student needs assistance, the item is incorrect.
STRONG PASS	The student meets the goals on all subtests and has attained the desired fluency. Proceed to Unit 14.
WEAK PASS	The student meets the goals on 3 out of 4 subtests and/or fails to attain the desired fluency. Proceed to Unit 14 with added practice, or provide Extra Practice in Unit 13, and/or provide a Jell-Well Review.
NO PASS	The student fails to meet the goal on 2 or more subtests. Provide Extra Practice lessons and retest, and/or provide a Jell-Well Review.

Certificate of Achievement

This certifies that

_____ ,

on this _____ day of _____ , _____ ,

has successfully completed

Read Well Unit 13

Sounds Mastered: s, e, ee, m, a, d, th, n, t, w, i, Th, h, c, r, ea

Words Mastered: I, see, I'm, me, am, Sam, mam, seem, sad, seed, mad, add, dad, said, seeds, seems, the, Nan, man, sees, Sams, an, and, than, seen, deed, sand, need, Dan, needs, at, sat, meet, meets, that, mat, ant, ants, was, Ann, we, weed, weeds, sweet, Nat, Dee, tan, in, it, sit, this, did, Tim, wind, that's, miss, win, mist, mints, tin, teen, sits, as, has, is, his, with, Dad's, dim, had, hand, hat, he, heed, hid, him, mint, mitt, Sam's, swim, swims, hasn't, isn't, wasn't, can, can't, Cass, cat, cat's, deeds, didn't, hadn't, hats, heeds, hiss, hit, miss, Nat's, scat, swiss, Tam, tee hee, want, wants, cats, dam, deer, eat, ham, hams, hear, heat, meat, mid, near, neat, ram, ran, rat, rats, read, rear, rid, seat, Sid, swam, sweets, Tad, three, tram, treat, tree

Personal Goal Setting

I would like to be able to:

_____

I can work on my goal by.

_____

My teacher will tell me when he or she notices me working on my goal.

Date _____   Student Signature _____

Teacher Signature _____

◆◆ ① SMOOTH AND BUMPY BLENDING

Select from Blending Cards 1–27 for review.

◆◆ ② STRETCH AND SHRINK

can-caaannn-can	What *can* we do? (We *can* [read].)
ran-rrraaannn-ran	The children *ran* a race.
rat-rrraaat-rat	What rhymes with "rat"? ([Cat])

③ SOUND DICTATION

Have students write each sound, then check and correct.

/rrr/ at the beginning of "rabbit" with small letter r

/c/ at the beginning of "cat" with small letter c

/eaeaea/ as in "eagle" with small letters e and a

◆◆ ④ WORD DICTATION

Have students count the sounds in each word with their fingers, identify and write each sound, and then read the word.

can	What *can* we do? (We *can* [read].)
ran	The children *ran* a race.
rat	What rhymes with "*rat*"? ([Cat])

The first word is "can." What *can* we do? (We *can* [read].)

We're going to count the sounds in "can."

Tell me the first sound. **Hold up one finger.** (/c/)

Repeat with /aaa/ and /nnn/.

How many sounds are in "can"? (Three)

Tell me the first sound. (/c/) Write it.

Repeat with /aaa/ and /nnn/.

Do Smooth Blending. (/caaannn/) **Read the word.** (can)

What *can* we do? (We *can* [read].)

Repeat with "ran" and "rat."

⑤ POSSESSIVE 'S

- Have students sound out each word, then read the phrase. (Remind students that they sound out words with the apostrophe just like they sound out other words.)
- Repeat practice, mixing group and individual turns, independent of your voice.

⑥ SOUNDING OUT SMOOTHLY

⑦ TRICKY WORDS

⑧ DAILY STORY READING

Proceed to Extra Practice Activity 1.

- Have students read each sentence from the book.
- Repeat, mixing group and individual turns, independent of your voice.

⑨ EXTRA PRACTICE ACTIVITY 1—CHECKOUT OPPORTUNITY

Have students fold, color, and read the book.

◆◆ For ELLs and children with language delays, provide repeated and extended practice with the language patterns. See page 10 for tips.

58

UNIT 13 EXTRA PRACTICE 1   Name_____

1. SMOOTH AND BUMPY BLENDING Select from Blending Cards 1–27 for review.

2. STRETCH AND SHRINK Have students orally
Stretch and Shrink, then use each word in a sentence.

3. SOUND DICTATION Have students write each sound, then check and correct:
/rrr/ at the beginning of "rabbit," /c/ at the beginning of "cat," /eaeaea/ as in "eagle."

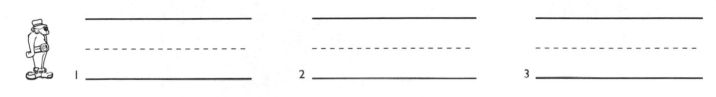

can-caaannn-can
ran-rrraaannn-ran
rat-rrraaat-rat

Do not have students read the words.

_____   _____   _____
- - - - -   - - - - -   - - - - -
_____   _____   _____

4. WORD DICTATION Have students count the sounds in each word, identify and write each sound, and then read the word: "can," "ran," and "rat."

_____   _____   _____
- - - - - -   - - - - - -   - - - - - -
1 _____   2 _____   3 _____

5. POSSESSIVE 'S Have students sound out each word, then read the phrase.

Tim's meat   Sam's ham   Nan's cat

6. SOUNDING OUT SMOOTHLY For each word, have students sound out the word in one smooth breath, and then read the word.

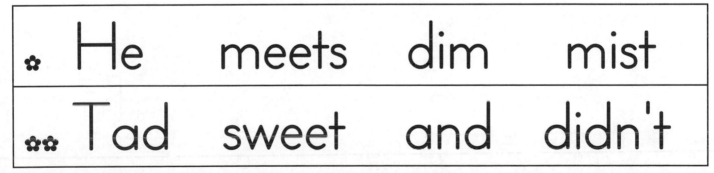

✿   He   meets   dim   mist

✿✿   Tad   sweet   and   didn't

7. TRICKY WORDS For each word, have students silently figure out the word, then read it aloud.

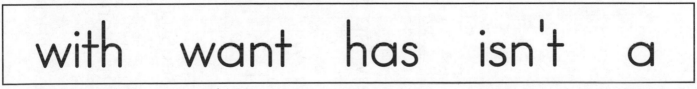

with   want   has   isn't   a

8. DAILY STORY READING

The  hid in a tree. 6

The wind said, "Www, 10

www, www." 12

The  wants a treat. 17

He sees a sweet treat. 22

Mmm, mmm, mmm, 25

sweet treats! 27

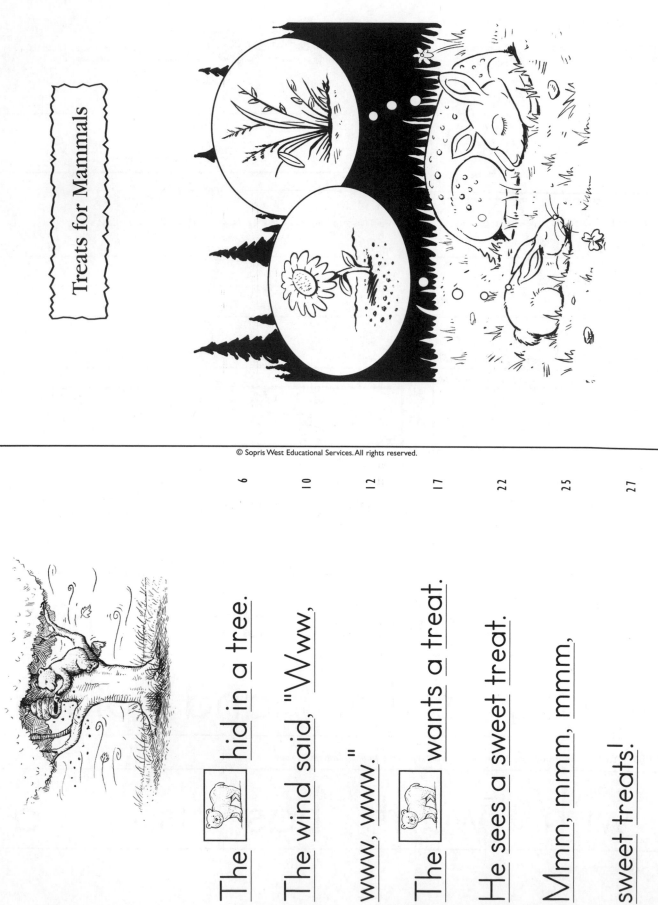

Treats for Mammals

3

6

11

15

19

23

26

28

See the deer.

See the 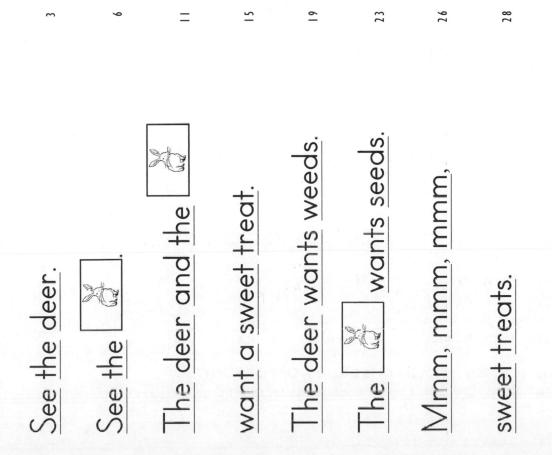.

The deer and the

want a sweet treat.

The deer wants weeds.

The wants seeds.

Mmm, mmm, mmm,

sweet treats.

1

◆◆ ❶ SMOOTH AND BUMPY BLENDING

Select from Blending Cards 1–27 for review.

◆◆ ❷ STRETCH AND SHRINK

eat-eaeaeat-eat	When I'm hungry, I need to . . . (*eat*).
tree-trrreeee-tree	The bear is up in the . . . (*tree*).
deer-deeeerrr-deer	An animal with antlers is a *deer*.

❸ SOUND DICTATION

Have students write each sound, then check and correct.

/eaeaea/ at the beginning of "eagle" with small letters <u>e</u> and <u>a</u>

/RRR/ at the beginning of "Rabbit" with capital letter <u>R</u>

/aaa/ at the beginning of "ant" with small letter <u>a</u>

> **CAUTION**
>
> Your children may not need Extra Practice. If in doubt, assess students and include Extra Practice only if needed.

HAVE STUDENTS CHECK AND CORRECT.

◆◆ ❹ WORD DICTATION

Have students count the sounds in each word with their fingers, identify and write each sound, and then read the word.

eat	When I'm hungry, I need to . . . (*eat*).
tree	The bear is up in the . . . (*tree*).
deer	An animal with antlers is a *deer*.

The first word is "eat." When I'm hungry, I need to . . . (*eat*).

We're going to count the sounds in "eat."

Tell me the first sound. **Hold up one finger.** (/eaeaea/)

Tell me the next sound. **Hold up two fingers.** (/t/)

How many sounds are in "eat"? (Two)

Tell me the first sound. (/eaeaea/) Write it with the letters <u>e</u> and <u>a</u>.

Tell me the next sound. (/t/) Write it.

Do Smooth Blending. (/eaeaeat/) Read the word. (eat)

When I'm hungry, I need to . . . (*eat*).

Repeat with "tree" and "deer."

❺ ACCURACY/FLUENCY BUILDING

- For each column, have students say any underlined part, then read the word.
- Have students read the whole column.
- Repeat practice on each column, building accuracy first and then fluency.

❻ TRICKY WORDS

Repeat practice, mixing group and individual turns, independent of your voice.

❼ DAILY STORY READING

Proceed to Extra Practice Activity 2.

- Have students read each sentence.
- Repeat, mixing group and individual turns, independent of your voice.

❽ EXTRA PRACTICE ACTIVITY 2—CHECKOUT OPPORTUNITY

As you listen to individuals read the story, have students color the picture.

◆◆ For ELLs and children with language delays, provide repeated and extended practice with the language patterns. See page 10 for tips.

Name _____

1. SMOOTH AND BUMPY BLENDING Select from Blending Cards 1–27 for review.

2. STRETCH AND SHRINK Have students orally Stretch and Shrink, then use each word in a sentence.

3. SOUND DICTATION Have students write each sound, then check and correct: /eaeaea/ as in "eagle," /RRR/ at the beginning of "Rabbit," /aaa/ at the beginning of "ant."

eat-eaeaeat-eat
tree-trrreeee-tree
deer-deeeerrr-deer

Do not have students read the words.

4. WORD DICTATION Have students count the sounds in each word, identify and write each sound, and then read the word: "eat," "tree," and "deer."

1 _____   2 _____   3 _____

5. ACCURACY/FLUENCY BUILDING In each column, have students say any underlined part, then read each word. Next, have students read the column.

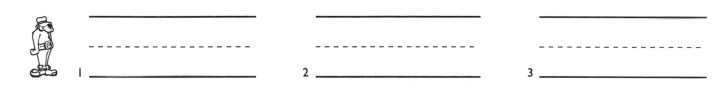

♥	♥♥	♥♥♥
T<u>im</u>	th<u>ree</u>	r<u>ea</u>d
him	tr<u>ee</u>	rear
swim	tr<u>ea</u>t	hear
sw<u>am</u>	sw<u>ee</u>t	near
ham	m<u>ea</u>t	deer

6. TRICKY WORDS For each word, have students silently figure out the word, then read it aloud.

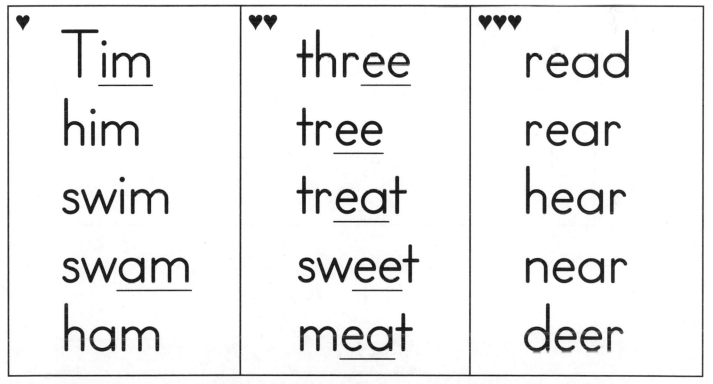

with   hasn't   a   said   was

7. DAILY STORY READING

Name_____

FLUENCY PASSAGE

Tim the

This is Tim.   3

He is a 🐻.   7

Tim wants meat.   10

He wants ham.   13

The ham is near that tree.   19

Tim wants to eat, eat, eat.   25

My goal is to read with 0–2 errors. This is what I did:

Have students read the sentences. Time individual students for 30 seconds; mark errors. To determine words correct per minute (wcpm), count words read in 30 seconds, subtract errors, multiply times two, and record on the chart. If student completes the passage in less than 30 seconds, have him or her return to the top and continue reading. (Repeated readings may be completed with older students, assistants, or parents.)

Reading	1st	2nd	3rd	4th
Errors				
Words/ 30 seconds				
wcpm				

64

1 STORYBOOK DECODING REVIEW

For each row, mix group and individual turns, independent of your voice.

2 SOLO STORY REVIEW—UNITS 10 AND 11

• Guide student reading, gradually increasing rate.

• Mix group and individual turns on the stories, independent of your voice.

• Repeat practice. While one student reads, have others track the text with their fingers and whisper read.

> **CAUTION**
> Your children may not need Extra Practice 3 and 4. If in doubt, assess students and include Extra Practice only if needed.

3 EXTRA PRACTICE ACTIVITY 3—CHECKOUT OPPORTUNITY

• Have students cut out the Letter Cards and arrange them on the Letter Card Grid to create the words "ran," "rat," "can," "cat," "eat," "read," and "near" in the blank row at the top of the page.

• Have students arrange and glue the letters in the remaining rows to create "can, "ran," and "rat." (While students are gluing letters, listen to individuals read a Solo Story.)

Challenge Activity: With the remaining letters, have students make a word in the blank row.

---

1 DECODING PRACTICE 4 REVIEW

For each row, mix group and individual turns, independent of your voice.

2 SOLO STORY REVIEW—UNITS 12 AND 13

• Guide student reading, gradually increasing rate and emphasizing expression.

• Mix group and individual turns on the stories, independent of your voice.

• Repeat practice. (While one student reads, have others track the text with their fingers and whisper read.)

3 EXTRA PRACTICE ACTIVITY 4—CHECKOUT OPPORTUNITY

• Have students cut out the Memory Cards. (While students are cutting out their cards, listen to individuals read a Solo Story.)

• Once the cards have been cut out, have the group or pairs of students play Memory.

Using one set of cards, spread the cards out in rows with the words facing down.

Have students take turns. Each time a card is turned over, have the group or pair identify the word.

If the words match, have students set the pair off to the side.

If the words do not match, have students turn the cards back over and try again.

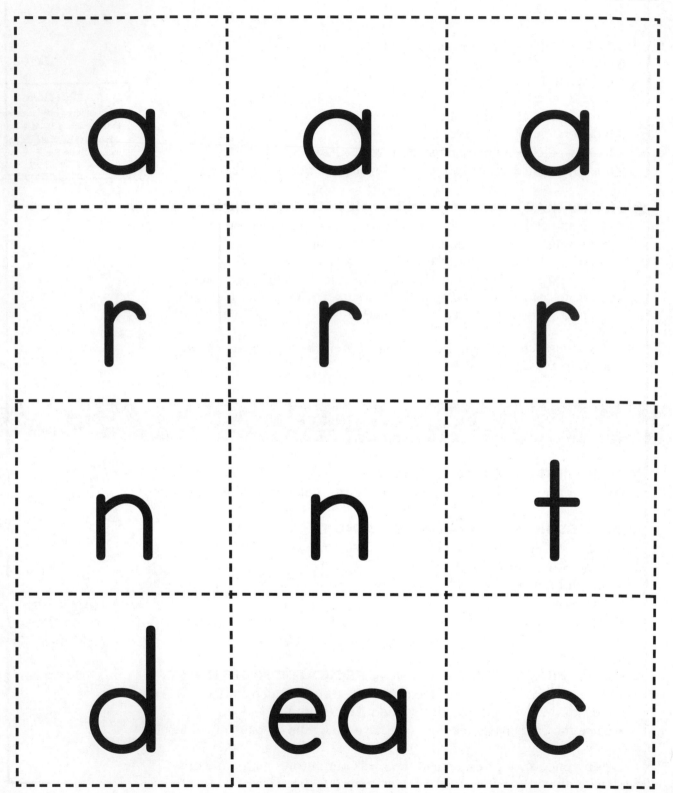

Name_____

Letter Card Grid

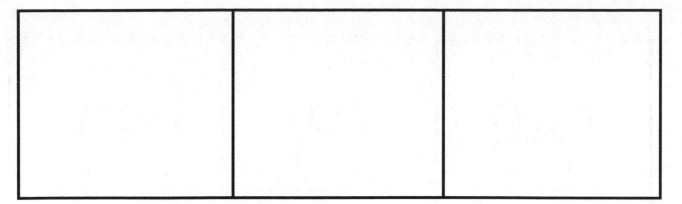

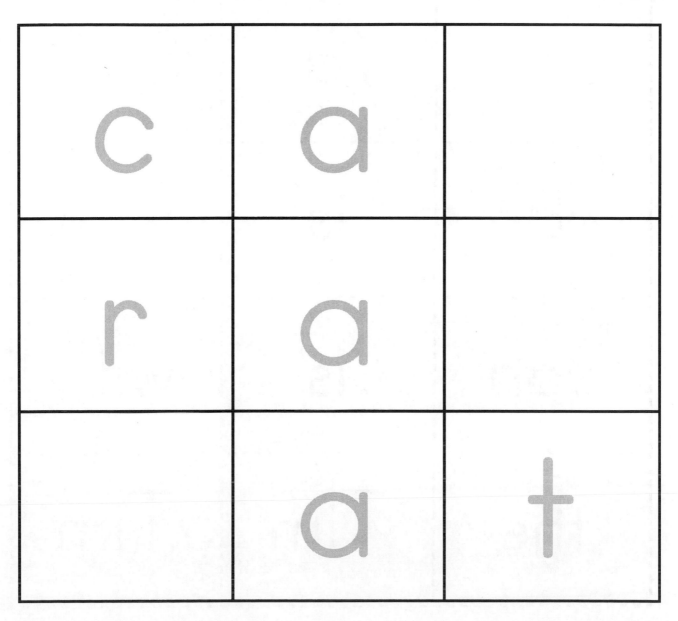

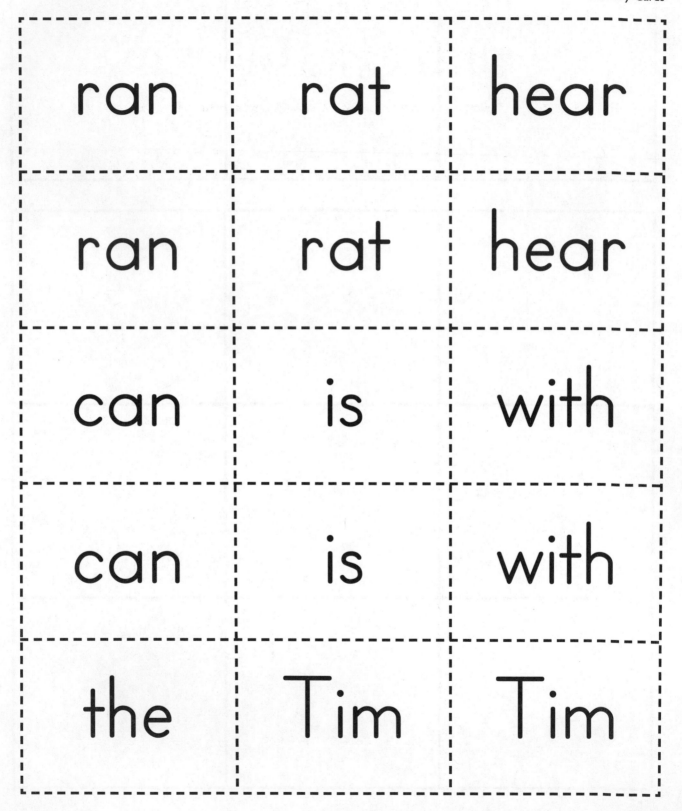

ran	rat	hear
ran	rat	hear
can	is	with
can	is	with
the	Tim	Tim

Note: The Memory Cards can also be used to create sentences. Also, please note there is no match for the word "the."

68